T0195808

language arts *for* gifted students

a
GIFTED CHILD TODAY
reader

language arts *for* gifted students

edited by
susan k. johnsen
and
james kendrick

Routledge
Taylor & Francis Group

NEW YORK AND LONDON

First published 2005 by Prufrock Press Inc.

Published 2021 by Routledge
605 Third Avenue, New York, NY 10017
2 Park Square, Milton Park, Abingdon, Oxon OX14 4RN

Routledge is an imprint of the Taylor & Francis Group, an informa business

© 2005 by Taylor & Francis

Library of Congress Cataloging-in-Publication Data

Language arts for gifted children /
edited by Susan K. Johnsen and James Kendrick.
     p. cm.—(A gifted child today reader)
Includes bibliographical references.
ISBN 1-59363-165-0
   1. Language arts—United States. 2. Gifted children—Education
  —United States. 3. Gifted children—Books and reading—United States.
  I. Johnsen, Susan K. II. Kendrick, James, 1974– . III. Series.
  LB1576.L2948 2005
  371.95'36--dc22

                                               2005018783

ISBN 13: 978-1-59363-165-9 (pbk)

contents

Overview

These articles from *Gifted Child Today* were selected specifically for the teacher who is searching for ways to serve students who are gifted in English/language arts. This overview provides a brief summary of the authors' major concepts covered in each of the chapters, including (a) characteristics of students who are gifted in English/language arts, (b) factors that contribute to their underachievement, (c) identification of students gifted in English/language arts, (d) qualities of teachers who are effective in working with these gifted students, (e) strategies for working with parents of gifted students, (f) attributes of a differentiated curriculum including multicultural components, and (g) specific strategies for teaching gifted students in language arts classrooms.

Using Renzulli's definition, Vosslamber describes the gifted reader as one who is above average, task-committed, and creative. Some of these students learn to read early, but not all early readers are gifted (Vosslamber, p. 5). Students who are gifted in English/language arts discern the author's purpose, anticipate layers of meaning, and use prior knowledge to make connections between the present text and previous experiences (Seney; Vosslamber). They delight in the world of language (Alber, Martin, & Gammill), have advanced vocabularies, and are able to "turn words into images, images to symbols, and symbols to personal reality" (Black, pp. 22–23). They are frequently voracious readers, reading as many as three to four times as many books as average children (Seney; Vosslamber). Through their reading, they satisfy their own curiosity, building their knowledge at a depth that is often beyond what is covered in the classroom (Seney).

Factors that may contribute to underachievement among gifted readers are the home and school environments (Vosslamber). For example, students who are from an economically or a socially disadvantaged background may not have access to books. On the other hand, those from an enriched background may be pacified by too much entertainment (e.g., TV, video games). If English is a second language, the gift may also be masked by language difficulties. At school, the curriculum may create underachieving gifted readers if available literature is too "high pitched" emotionally or "too easy or immature" (Vosslamber, p. 6). Gifted students wanting to fit in may not show their ability to peers or teachers. Vosslamber provides a poignant example of a 5-year-old boy who is referred to the school psychologist for his inability to learn to read. During assessment, the startled psychologist discovered that the child had been reading the *Encyclopedia Britannica* at home!

Vosslamber suggests that schools use multiple assessments and sources to identify students gifted in English/language arts. These assessments may include formal objective measures such as achievement and intelligence tests and informal subjective measures such as running records, observations, nominations, self-assessments, and teacher-made tests. Teachers, parents, and students are all valuable sources of information during the identification process.

Teachers who are effective in working with students who are gifted in English/language arts are diligent in making sure that appropriate literature and information are available (Seney), and they provide a variety of choices among general categories of literature (Alber, Martin, & Gammill; Seney). They need to read any recommended books first in order to understand not only how they relate to the students' interests, but also to the community and its values (Kingore; Frey; Seney). In this way, they may avoid issues related to censorship (Seney). Teachers will want to provide alternative ways for concepts to be explored and developed (Black), sometimes creating a structure by modeling and demonstrating the basic story, actions, dialogue, and characterization (Johnson). Teachers need to be skilled in questioning techniques to encourage discussion and reflection about the students' reading experiences (Black; Ford, Howard, & Harris; Frey; Johnson; Kingore; Polette; Seney).

Seney provides guidelines for working with parents to avoid challenges to literary choices. Some of his suggestions include providing parents with a list of novels at the beginning of the year, defining the learning goals for each novel, encouraging parents to read the novels and discuss them with their children, and having parents suggest alternatives if there are any problems.

VanTassel-Baska, Johnson, Hughes, and Boyce suggest that a "focused, high-powered, and integrated curriculum intervention in the language arts of even a relatively short duration can bring about important changes in students' performance" (cited by Frey, p. 153). Such curricula are challenging, integrative, and exploratory (Frey), and they expose students to quality literature (Frey; Seney). They cover a broad range of concepts and contexts and incorporate novel products and cultural material so that students may independently explore their interests in depth (Alber, Martin, & Gammill). Multicultural content may be successfully infused into the curriculum by integrating Bloom's Cognitive Taxonomy into Banks' Multicultural Framework (Ford, Howard, & Harris). In this way, gifted students can "learn to become pluralistic in their thought, behavior, and affect" (Ford, Howard, & Harris, p. 45). Teachers should select literature with authors of merit, well-developed characters, thought-provoking problem situations, issues or personal needs with which gifted students can identify, and themes that represent diverse backgrounds (Kingore).

The authors recommend a variety of strategies for teaching students who are gifted in English/language arts:

1. The integration of drama into literature introduces gifted students to famous playwrights and assists them in creating their own scripts (Johnson; O'Day; Winstead).

2. The study of literary masters gives gifted students a method for discovering their own voices and inspires written expression (Alber, Martin, & Gammill).
3. Using a journal to examine parallels and relationships, the gifted student uses literature to understand themselves as individuals (Black).
4. Middle school and high school students may read novels that deal with censorship to understand issues in pursuing controversial topics (Seney).
5. In developing critical reading and writing skills, the teacher may guide gifted students using the RITE (read, interrogate, tell, explore) process (Polette).
6. Considering the students' preferences, language can be developed as by-products of drama, dance, music, and art (Black).
7. A writers' workshop may be helpful in encouraging a discussion of literature and drafts of poems, short stories, or essays (Frey).
8. Storytelling creates musical and pictorial images that help students create an ear for language and the sound and rhythm of words (Black).
9. If gifted readers have limited writing skills, they may develop a character analysis using mobiles, summarize plots in picture form, develop characters using speech bubbles, and use nonfiction material to conduct basic research (Vosslamber).

We want to thank these authors for their contributions to this book. We hope this book assists you in teaching students who are gifted in English/language arts.

Susan K. Johnsen
James Kendrick
Editors

Gifted Readers

who are they, and how can they
be served in the classroom?

by **Andrea Vosslamber**

any of us may not perceive a link between the traditional tale of "The Three Little Pigs" and R. L. Stein's *Goosebumps* series, but Ivan, a 6-year-old in my classroom, did. I had used "The Three Little Pigs," along with other traditional tales, to point out the introduction, complication, and resolution structure of simple narrative. Ivan's mother spoke to me after the series of lessons and reported that her son had come out with a surprising comment. Having recently been to South Africa, where his grandmother had read him one of the *Goosebumps* books, he had forged a link. He told his mother that he had finally worked out what was "wrong" with the *Goosebumps* series: They had an introduction and a complication, but no resolution! Quite an insight for a 6-year-old. His behavior showed evidence of an advanced reading ability.

The Gifted Reader

Who is a gifted reader? In order to answer this question, we need to define what we mean by *gifted* and what we mean by *reading* (Jackson, Donaldson, & Cleland, 1988). A well-known definition of gifted was put forward by Joseph Renzulli, who posited that there are three clusters of human traits that interact in the gifted. The traits are as follows and are represented by three interlinking circles:

- *above-average ability*: This does not mean high IQ, but "a wide field of general and specific ability";
- *task commitment*: "the capacity for sustained motivation, dedicated practice, and excellence in the development of ideas and products"; and
- *creativity*: "involves fluency, flexibility and originality of thought, the ability to produce novel and effective solutions to problems, and to create clever and original products" (McAlpine, 1996, p. 35).

Reading may be defined as simply being able to decode text. However children who fall into the category *hyperlexic* are accurate decoders, even being able to decode pseudowords, yet they have very poor comprehension (Jackson, Donaldson, & Cleland, 1988). Usually, however, reading is associated with the ability to comprehend, as well as decode. In discussing gifted readers, a bottom up definition of reading will be applied, namely that reading is the ability to comprehend the message the author intended on the basis of accurate decoding ability (Adams & Bruck, 1993).

The gifted reader is one who evidences the three aspects of giftedness that Renzulli proposed (above-average ability, task commitment, and creativity) in the area of reading. Both cognitive and social/emotional behaviors of gifted readers may be explained within the framework of Renzulli's three rings. Cognitive behaviors refer to thinking processes, which are mainly found in the above-average ability ring, with the outcomes of these behaviors being within the task commitment ring. Social/emotional behaviors are the more emotional aspects of giftedness, which mainly arise within the creativity circle. However, just as there is overlap between Renzulli's rings, so there is overlap between the affective and cognitive realms. Thus, some social/emotional behaviors may arise in more than just the creativity circle and vice-versa.

Characteristics of the Gifted Reader

The gifted reader may evidence above-average ability, task commitment, and creativity in varied ways. Table 1 summarizes some of the more common indicators.

Above-Average Ability

Catron (1986) listed the specific skills that gifted readers possess, as opposed to those skills employed by average readers:

1. anticipation of meaning based on visual clues
   - punctuation, the use of commas to set off appositives;
   - syntax, the use of *however* to signal exceptions;
   - organizational patterns, such as cause and effect signaling the need to look for two related descriptions, circumstances, or facts;
2. use of prior knowledge and experience, personal identification, and reader purpose; and
3. awareness of the cognitive processing of text for information/concept gathering. Links are made between the present text and what the reader has previously read, and, as a result, concepts are formed or developed. (p. 136)

My pupil, Ivan, clearly was engaging in this process.

Some of these differences in comprehension, which separate the gifted from the average reader, can be seen in the results of research conducted by Fehrenbach (1991). Taking a group of gifted readers (identified by high intelligence, high language basic skills test results, and high reading comprehension results) and a group of average readers (identified by the same test measures, but with average results), she tested them by having each student read aloud an easy passage. Each student was instructed to verbalize his or her thoughts as often as he or she chose or at points indicated by asterisks after every few sentences. Any student who did not stop to comment at an asterisk was asked, "What are you thinking?" In the second session, the same procedure was followed with students reading a difficult passage. Her findings showed that gifted readers used six strategies signif-

---

Table 1. **Indicators of Gifted Reading Ability in Terms of Renzulli's Three-Ring Conception of Giftedness**

Indicators of Above-Average Ability

- Advanced IQ (Hartley, 1996)
- High scores on language achievement tests (Anderson Tollefson, & Gilbert, 1985; Hartley)
- Higher levels of reading than peers (Catron, 1986; Gaug, 1984; Hartley; Trezise, 1978)
- Large vocabulary (Catron; Greenlaw, 1986; Smith, 1991)
- Good memory of things read (Smith)
- Strong comprehension of texts (Smith)
- Early reading (Baskin & Harris, 1980; Cathcart, 1994; Halsted, 1988, 1990; Trezise, 1978)

Indicators of Task Commitment

- Long attention span (Ringler & Weber, 1984; Smith)
- Voracious reading (Halsted)
- Selection of high level reading materials (Ringler & Weber)
- Spontaneous reading of materials to prove/disprove points (Ringler & Weber)

Indicators of Creativity

- Complex thoughts and ideas (Smith)
- Good judgement and logic (Smith)
- Forms the relationships between concepts (Smith)
- Produce original ideas and products (Halsted; Smith)
- Appreciates beauty (Greenlaw)
- Sense of humor (Greenlaw)
- Divergent thinking (Catron; Halsted)
- Problem-solving strategies used to solve unanswered questions (Halsted)
- High level of sensitivity and empathy (McAlpine, 1996)
- Concern over moral and ethical issues and a strong sense of justice (McAlpine)
- Social leadership abilities (McAlpine)

---

icantly more often than average readers: rereading, inferring, analyzing text structure, watching or predicting, evaluating, and relating what is read to content area knowledge.

Many gifted children learn to read early, and while this may be a sign of giftedness, it is not always so. Some children who are hyperlexic do learn to read very early; but, because they have little or no comprehension, they are not termed gifted readers (Jackson, Donaldson, & Cleland, 1988). It is also noted that young gifted children do not necessarily learn to read early (Alvino, 1989), something Piaget also noted in his studies on the development of children (Polette, 1992). This may be the case even where young gifted children have participated in preschool programs designed to help them to learn to read early (Jackson & Cleland, 1982).

Task Commitment

Gifted readers often have voracious reading habits. Gifted readers may read into the night (Hartley, 1996) or read as many books as average-ability readers (Halsted, 1988). Reading fulfills an extra sense of urgency about "needing to know" that gifted children seem to have (Halsted). These reading behaviors are tied to the perception that reading is fun, and therefore it is a preferred activity (Anderson, Tollefson, & Gilbert, 1985).

Creativity (Divergent Thinking)

An interesting anecdote comes to mind in the area of divergent thinking. A 6-year-old whom I once taught came to me and asked if he could shut the door because the sixth-grade students in music were too loud. I replied that they were not really that noisy and that we needed the door open to keep the room cool. He replied, "Okay then, I guess I'll just have to think a bit louder."

On a cautionary note, much as the creative traits listed above may be evident in a gifted reader, one must be aware that they are not necessarily specific to gifted readers, nor will each gifted reader necessarily display all of these social/emotional behaviors.

Underachieving Gifted Readers

A group of children who may be gifted, but may not show above average ability or related task commitment behaviors, could be labeled as underachieving gifted students. Home life and school life can be contributing factors to these students' underachievement. They may be from an economically or socially disadvantaged background with little or no access to books (Baskin & Harris, 1980). In addition, English may be a second language, and therefore their giftedness may be masked by language difficulties (Cathcart, 1994). Conversely, they could be disadvantaged by a wealthy (or poor) background where too much entertainment (e.g. TV, video games, etc.) is provided that intellectually pacifies the child (Baskin & Harris). High expectations at home may lead to a perfectionism that inclines children not to try in order to avoid not meeting their own expectations (Halsted, 1988). In the affective realm, some gifted children may feel a sense of isolation due to their intense interest in subject matter that their peers do not understand (Trezise, 1978). This may result in their having to choose between fitting in with the group or showing their ability (Halsted, 1988).

School life can also be difficult for gifted readers. Children may be frustrated by the material provided because it is either too highly pitched emotionally for the child (Cathcart, 1994), or it may be far too easy or immature (Trezise, 1978). For example:

> A 5-year-old boy was referred to a psychologist for complete failure even to begin to learn to read. He just didn't seem to be interested. While he was being tested by the psychologist, the little boy was asked to give the names of some animals he knew. He promptly reeled off the Latin names of various extinct species. "Where did you learn all those?" asked the startled psychologist. "I read about them at home in the *Encyclopedia Britannica*," replied the five-year-old "reading failure." This highly gifted little boy, too polite to tell the teacher the books she offered him were too easy, had been labeled "backward" for months before this test revealed his true ability level. (Cathcart, p. 3)

We must be concerned as educators to have procedures in place to identify such children and to know how to put programs in place that will cater for their educational needs.

Teacher Identification

Some schools in New Zealand have a policy for gifted children that included identification procedures for children who have special abilities. Bethlehem College in Tauranga, New Zealand, has one such policy, which is comprehensive in scope.

Methods of identification must be wide in scope, inclusive in emphases, and relate to definitions and ensuing programs. To be successful, any identification process must start early, but be continuous (an ongoing process), be aware of cultural differences, use multiple methods, and recognize that achievement is not the only measure of ability. Thus, we need a balance between subjective and objective procedures. A multifaceted approach will make it less likely for a gifted student to be unnoticed. (Sanders, 1994, p. 2)

Drawing from these recommendations, a multifaceted identification procedure for gifted readers might include the following:

1. Talk to parents during enrollment about their child's language ability. Ask if the child can read and, if so, how he or she learned.

2. Be aware that certain methods of evaluating students may be inappropriate for certain cultures.

3. Use assessment practices, such as:
   - running records (Clay, 1985)—these are ongoing and routinely done;
   - record of skill mastery—early school records that show the rapid mastery of phonic skills may be indicators of gifted reading;
   - achievement test scores—assessments for reading vocabulary, listening comprehension, and reading comprehension;
   - self-made tests—these often concentrate on higher cognitive processing skills, such as analysis, synthesis, and evaluation (Clay, 1985);

- intelligence tests;
- title recognition test—in this test, the teacher constructs a list of book titles and asks the children to check all those that they know (Dymock, 1995), which may indicate voracious reading; and
- word recognition test.

4. Make informal teacher observations, including:
    - listen to the vocabulary the child uses—does he or she choose interesting words, or express him or herself very clearly?;
    - look for evidence of critical thinking—this may arise during class discussion time or during specific problem-solving activities;
    - look for evidence of thinking outside the box—this type of behavior may appear to be naughtiness, but it needs to be carefully considered and evaluated;
    - listen for a sense of humor, particularly humor that relies on puns;
    - listen for unusual questions, which may betray deep thought processes and connections; and
    - conduct language activities and look for interest and attentiveness in involvement in these activities.

5. Get input from others:
    - Talk to other teachers about their observations of the child. For young readers, this may include comments from the preschool teachers.
    - Peer nominations can be done directly or quite unobtrusively. They could be done using a teacher-designed form that asks questions such as "Who is the best reader in the class?"
    - Self-assessment can occur when children are asked to rate themselves as to their reading ability.
    - Parents are a vital source of information on their children's reading habits.

Classroom Programs

Identification is an important aspect of serving the gifted child, but is not an end in itself. To quote the Bethlehem policy, "The main purpose of identification is not so we can label children, but so we can effectively match children to appropriate learning tasks—both in the pace of learning and the level at which tasks are set" (as cited in Sanders, 1994, p. 2). The provision of special classroom programs is necessary if schools want to serve adequately those children who have high reading ability.

Enrichment vs. Acceleration

There are two main ways that gifted readers' needs are addressed in the classroom: enrichment or acceleration. Enrichment refers to "learning activities providing depth and breadth to regular teaching according to the child's abilities and needs" (Townsend, 1996, p. 362). Examples of enrichment activities involve children being given activities or resources that are more demanding than those given to their classmates. These could include "independent projects, mentors, learning centers, opportunities to use higher level thinking skills, and extension activities" (Townsend, p. 36.). Table 2 summarizes some of the advantages and disadvantages of enrichment.

As an alternative to enrichment, acceleration could be used. "Acceleration occurs when children are exposed to new content at an earlier age than other children or when they cover the same content in less time" (Townsend, 1996, p. 361). This can involve starting school early, skipping a class, starting university early, taking an advanced class, or compressing the curriculum. As with enrichment, acceleration also has advantages and disadvantages (see Table 3).

Given the advantages and disadvantages of both acceleration and enrichment, many scholars have advocated that both be used. "Enrichment and acceleration can complement each other and enable gifted readers to pursue their own interests in reading, develop higher level thinking skills, avoid boredom, and still master skills" (Gaug, 1984, p. 375).

Table 2. **Advantages and Disadvantages of Enrichment**

Advantages of Enrichment

- Avoids problems associated with overt labeling (Townsend, 1996). Children remain in their regular classes and have their individual needs met, just like all the other students.
- "Avoids a fragmented learning experience by keeping gifted and talented students connected—albeit horizontally—to the general classroom activities and topics of study" (Ministry of Education, 2000, p. 39).
- "May curb problems associated with intellectual frustration and boredom" (Ministry of Education, p. 39.).

Disadvantages of Enrichment

- "Often little more than busy work where children get more of the same" (Townsend, p. 367).
- "Often assumed to have the same purpose for all children and usually pays little attention to the specific nature of the abilities of gifted children" (Townsend, p. 367).
- "Often provided intermittently, or as a filler or one-off activity that provides relief from or contrast to regular classroom activities" (Townsend, p. 367).

Practical Outcomes for the Classroom

Bearing in mind Gaug's (1984) comments about using enrichment and acceleration in combination, how can gifted readers be served in the classroom? In considering these options, it must be remembered that there are individual differences in the gifted population (Hartley, 1996). These strategies should be selected according to the needs of the individual student. If a first- or second-grade child who can already read enters school, allow him or her to bypass the learning of decoding skills (Catron, 1986; Hartley, 1996) and instead emphasize comprehension skills, which may include critical reading skills and creative reading (Trezise, 1978).

There is a danger that young capable readers might be held back from more advanced work due to their poor writing ability (Trezise, 1978). If harder books have accompanying workbook exercises that the child cannot master because of lack of

Table 3. **Advantages and Disadvantages of Acceleration**

Advantages of Acceleration

- Some research findings show greater academic achievement for gifted children who were accelerated, compared to those who were not (Gaug, 1984).
- Provides mental stimulation and opportunities to interact with like minds (Ministry of Education, 2000).

Disadvantages of Acceleration

- For the gifted reader, stories and activities at a higher class level could be inappropriate, "involving situations beyond students' emotional and social level" (Gaug, p. 374).
- Younger students may feel isolated and different in a class with older peers (Ministry of Education).

fine motor skill development, invent and prepare different activities that will extend them without requiring writing skills. Such activities might include:

- character analysis using mobiles;
- plot summarization of individual chapters in picture form;
- plot summarization of a number of chapters in picture form;
- character development through a series using a speech bubble and a decorated story character;
- character development through a single story using pictures; and
- using nonfiction material to conduct basic research, resulting in the production of a poster.

Young, competent readers should be given chapter books to read (Halsted, 1988), and they may benefit from being promoted to a higher class. As gifted readers mature, they will benefit from instruction in advanced comprehension and thinking skills. As a means of developing higher thinking skills in all learners, Bloom's (1956) taxonomy might be used as a guide. For most classroom programs, the majority of instruction being given is in the knowledge and comprehension areas. In all programs, the higher levels should be emphasized (Ministry of Education, 2000, p. 49). Therefore, the gifted program should focus mainly on evaluation, synthesis, and analysis, rather than knowledge, comprehension, and application, which are less challenging for learners.

In order to help students function at the higher levels of comprehension, high-level tests should be used to uncover areas of deficient skill (Catron, 1986). Once the particular strengths and weaknesses of the pupils have been identified, they can be addressed in day-to-day classroom work.

Discussion about books is one way that higher comprehension skills can be enhanced. After students have read a passage, teachers can pose questions such as "What inferences can be made on the basis of the reading you did?," "What were the main ideas and the subordinate ideas?," "What about the prevailing tone and mood of the selection?," "What can you say about the author's biases or his or her purposes?," and "Can you speculate about the characters' motivations?" (Trezise, 1978, p. 745). Discussion groups could be selected across grade levels in the school. A teacher who is also interested in reading and higher cognitive skills could facilitate discussion about books the students had read, deliberately aiming at the upper levels of Bloom's taxonomy (Halsted, 1988). Another idea is to choose books on a common theme (e.g., *Island of the Blue Dolphins* [O'Dell, 1966], *The Iceberg Hermit* [Roth, 1974], *Ice Trap!* [Hooper & Robertson, 2000], and *Robinson Crusoe* [Defoe & Heller, 1998]) and have the students discuss these from the standpoint of qualities needed for survival and make appropriate narrative and thematic links among the texts.

Creative and inquiry reading are other ways of encouraging higher thinking skills. Creative reading involves "synthesis, integration, application, and extension of ideas. A story may be dramatized through the use of music, dance, or visual arts, or a character or theme may be developed in a new and different way" (Catron, 1986, p. 139). Inquiry reading involves students carefully formulating a question that will need to be researched for several weeks. After researching their questions, the students choose a creative way to present their findings (Cassidy, 1981).

Good literature is a must for gifted readers as they develop their higher cognitive skills. Gifted students will not necessarily choose high-quality literature, so they need to be directed to it by discerning adults (Baskin & Harris, 1980; Hartley, 1996). There are many resources available that summarize the various lists of classical literature. Halsted (1988) provided a list of criteria for books that encourage intellectual stimulation, including a high level of language, pronunciation guides, good use of literary devices, and many more. Baskin and Harris, among others, identified a list of books that meet Halsted's (1988) criteria and included a short synopsis of plots. Good literature is also necessary for vocabulary development (Hartley). Boothby (1986) listed books that can be used to enhance the vocabulary of gifted children by studying connotations, figurative language, and etymology.

Gifted readers' social/emotional needs should also be served in the school program. Bibliotherapy is the term given to the use of literature to help students deal with emotional difficulties they might be facing (Halsted, 1988). Halsted has provided a list of books that might help gifted children deal with problems related to establishing an identity, being alone, getting along with others, and using their abilities.

Conclusion

Teachers need to be concerned about identifying gifted children's abilities so they can provide suitable programs to nurture such abilities. Ongoing, comprehensive identification procedures may help with the recognition of above-average ability, task commitment, and creativity in the area of reading. Using a combination of enrichment and acceleration, specialized programs can then be put in place to meet both the cognitive and social/ emotional needs of high-ability readers.

References

Adams, M. J., & Bruck, M. (1993). Word recognition: The interface of educational policies and scientific research. *Reading and Writing: An Interdisciplinary Journal, 5,* 113–139.

Alvino, J. A. (1989). *Parents' guide to raising a gifted child*. New York: Ballantine Books.

Anderson, M. A., Tollefson, N. A., & Gilbert, E. C. (1985). Giftedness and reading: A cross-sectional view of differences in reading attitudes and behaviors. *Gifted Child Quarterly, 29*, 186–89.

Baskin, B. H., & Harris, K. H. (1980). *Books for the gifted child*. New York: Bowker.

Bloom, B. S. (Ed.). (1956). *Taxonomy of educational objectives: Handbook 1: The cognitive domain*. London: Longmans.

Boothby, P. R. (1986). Creative and critical reading for the gifted. *Reading Teacher, 33*, 674–676.

Cassidy, J. (1981). Inquiry reading for the gifted. *Reading Teacher, 35*, 17–21.

Cathcart, R. (1994). *They're not bringing my brain out*. Auckland, New Zealand: REACH.

Catron, R. M. (1986). Developing the potential of the gifted reader. *Theory Into Practice, 25*, 134–40.

Clay, M. M. (1985). *The early detection of reading difficulties* (3rd ed.). Auckland, New Zealand: Heinemann.

Defoe, D., & Heller, J. (1998). *Robinson Crusoe*. London: Dorling Kindersley.

Dymock, S. (1995). Measuring print exposure in New Zealand classrooms: The title recognition test. *Set, 1*(11).

Fehrenbach, C. R. (1991). Gifted/average readers: Do they use the same reading strategies? *Gifted Child Quarterly, 35*, 125–127.

Gaug, M. A. (1984). Reading acceleration and enrichment in the elementary grades. *Reading Teacher, 37*, 372–376.

Greenlaw, M. J. (1986). Literature for use with gifted children. *Childhood Education, 62*, 381–386.

Halsted, J. W. (1988). *Guiding gifted readers*. Dayton: Ohio Psychology Press.

Hartley, M. (1996). Reading and literature. In D. McAlpine & R. Moltzen (Eds.), *Gifted and talented: New Zealand perspectives* (pp. 253–272). Palmerston North, New Zealand: Educational Research and Development Center, Massey University.

Hooper, M., & Robinson, M. P. (2000). *Ice trap!: Shackleton's incredible expedition*. London: Frances Lincoln.

Jackson, N. E., & Cleland, L. N. (1982). *Skill patterns of precocious readers*. Paper presented at the annual meeting of the American Educational Research Association, New York.

Jackson, N. E., Donaldson, G. W., & Cleland, L. N. (1988). The structure of precocious reading ability. *Journal of Educational Psychology, 80*, 234–43.

McAlpine, D. (1996). Concepts and definitions. In D. McAlpine & R. Moltzen (Eds.), *Gifted and talented: New Zealand perspectives.* Palmerston North, New Zealand: Educational Research and Development Center, Massey University.

Ministry of Education. (2000). *Gifted and talented students: Meeting their needs in New Zealand schools.* Wellington, New Zealand: Learning Media.

O'Dell, S. (1966). *Island of the blue dolphins.* New York: Dell.

Polette, N. J. (1992). *Brain power through picture books.* London: McFarland.

Ringler, H., & Weber, C. K. (1984). *A language-thinking approach to reading.* Toronto, Ontario, Canada: Harcourt.

Roth, A. J. (1974). *The iceberg hermit.* New York: Four Winds Press.

Sanders, M. (1994). *Bethlehem College policy on learners with special abilities.* Tauranga, New Zealand: Bethlehem College.

Smith, C. B. (1991). Literature for gifted and talented. *Reading Teacher, 44,* 608–609.

Townsend, M. A (1996). Enrichment and acceleration: Lateral and vertical perspectives in provisions for gifted and talented children. In D. McAlpine & R. Moltzen (Eds.), *Gifted and talented: New Zealand perspectives* (pp. 361–176). Palmerston North, New Zealand: Educational Research and Development Center, Massey University.

Trezise, R. L. (1978). What about a reading programme for the gifted? *Reading Teacher, 31,* 742–747.

Using Literature With Gifted Students

chapter 1

Harry Potter
enchantment for all seasons

by **Sharon Black**

aria, age 7, has recently immigrated with her family to the United States from South Africa. She is making a variety of adjustments in her life, which include attending a U.S. school and learning to play the violin. Maria sometimes feels bombarded at having to cope with the many changes and new opportunities at the same time. She loves the Harry Potter books. The adventures are exciting, no matter what kinds of experiences or adaptations she is going through.

• • •

When 10-year-old Kassie's mom offered to buy her the Harry Potter books, Kassie wasn't particularly interested. She read almost anything she could get her hands on, but she didn't want to read a book about a boy. Grudgingly Kassie agreed to read part of *Harry Potter and the Sorcerer's Stone* to please her mother. But, somewhere between Privet Drive and Hogwarts, Kassie's gifted imagination was hooked. During the next 18 months, she read all the Potter books five times each. Kassie avoided the first Harry Potter movie; she knew it wouldn't portray the book as she had imagined it—and it didn't. When she was dragged to the movie via a friend's birthday party, Kassie came home and immediately began to reread the book. "I have to get my imagination back," she wailed.

• • •

Somewhat ironically, Sally, at 23, met Harry Potter on her return from a year and a half in England. She had heard of him in his native land, but Sally had been too busy teaching the children of various Privet Drives to visit Hogwarts. She had sung with neglected children to bring a little magic into their hearts before they went home to be, like Harry, ignored and brushed aside—or worse. She had sung and played her violin for the neglected elderly, trying to find the magic that would give them a reason to keep on with their lives. Like her violin student, Kassie, she allowed herself to be talked into reading a little Harry Potter. And, like Kassie, she couldn't stop. Sally found in the Dursleys, the Weasleys, the inhabitants of Gryffindor and Slytherin, and even in a few of the Hogwarts professors some of the mirth and the suffering she'd seen in the cities and villages of England and the United States. "I see both good and evil in the adventures of Harry Potter," she reflected, "and I cheer when I see the good win."

Three gifted individuals—facing different conflicts, different questions, different developmental needs. On the surface, they seem to be unified only in their love and talent for music, in the fact that the younger girls are Sally's violin students, and in the fact that all of them enjoy Harry Potter. Yet, all are struggling to define and understand who they are and how they can maximize the potentials within them. Each has found some answers in Harry Potter. Why Harry? Why Privet Drive? Why Hogwarts?

In his classic work on fairy tales, psychiatrist and literary analyst Bruno Bettelheim (1976) wrote (long before the advent of Harry Potter), "If we hope to live not just from moment to moment, but in true consciousness of our existence, then our greatest need and most difficult achievement is to find meaning in our lives" (p. 2). Bettelheim continued by saying that, next to the influence of the parents, the most potent force for this search for meaning is one's cultural heritage and that, "when children are young, it is literature that carries such information best" (p. 4), particularly those stories that allow the child "to bring his [or her] inner house into order, and on that basis [to] create order in his [or her] life" (p. 5).

Harry Potter is a story that can meet such needs, particularly for the gifted, with their vivid imaginations, their need to understand themselves as individuals who often stand apart, and their drive to make sense of a universe that can be a complicated mix of good and evil, ethical and unethical, humane and cruel. Fantasy in general, and Harry Potter in particular, can be a valuable tool for (a) engaging gifted imaginations, (b) helping the gifted to understand better their personal needs and conflicts, and (c) providing them the tools to reason through deeper meanings of the universe in which they live.

This chapter focuses on the enchantment of Harry Potter in the development of gifted imagination, self- concept, and worldview in light of Bettelheim's seminal work, *The Uses of Enchantment* (1976). As the processes are discussed, suggestions to guide parents and teachers in facilitating them are included, as well. Sally, Kassie, and Maria, though real people with real personalities and needs, are viewed according to the needs and characteristics they share with other gifted individuals. Sally is the author's daughter; the others, as Sally's students, have been available to observe. The treatment is, of course, qualitative, and if it is at times less than detached, it is because it is difficult to be detached when it comes to those you know and love.

The Uses of Imagery and Imagination

Many, if not most, gifted children take naturally to imagery, particularly metaphor. Fantasy is well suited to the gifted child who thinks in this fashion, as fantasy is a "metaphorical mode." Through fantasy, "metaphorical images become the vehicle by which [experience, ideas, and feelings] are rendered" (Gooderham, 1995, p. 173). The child resonates with the images (Gooderham), personalizes them, and finds within them the raw material for his or her own daydreams (Bettelheim, 1976) and eventual restructuring of personal reality.

Imaginative restructuring can, of course, take place on many levels. As a second grader, Maria wants to play beautiful violin music, but methodically practicing finger positions and bow arm movement are not among her most cherished daydreams. However, when Sally plays for Maria the theme from the Harry Potter movie, Maria sees Privet Drive, a magical train ride, and a mysterious castle. When Sally makes up a practice game/chart based on Quidditch, the dangerous and exciting game Harry plays on a flying broomstick, Maria sees herself challenged, as Harry is, to work her hardest to develop her talent and reach her goals. Maria would still rather play outdoors than practice, but a little Potter-style imagination helps.

Imaginative involvement can be carried to an even higher level through writing—especially for gifted children who tend to be naturally interested in, and good at, expressing themselves with language. Children on Maria's level may start bringing a little Hogwarts into their world by inventing a new magical candy (comparable to Harry's Every Flavor Beans or Chocolate Frogs), thinking up their own spell or potion (as Hermione magically mends Harry's glasses), or creating a new magical creature (like the growling, snapping textbook Harry buys for his Magical Creatures class). To put themselves more distinctly into Harry's world, children could be directly challenged to make up their own adventure based on one of Harry's situations:

"You've just been given an invisibility cloak. Where will you go?"

"You've received a Nimbus 2000 flying broomstick for Christmas. What will you do?"

"You've just received authorization to become an animagus (someone who can turn into an animal at will). What will you become, and what will happen?"

Gifted children are natural storytellers, and to extend from the outrageous imagination of J. K. Rowling is irresistible.

Kassie, as a fifth grader, a little older and probably more highly gifted than Maria, does not need movie music or story prompts to help her find herself in Harry Potter's world. She has said she wouldn't carry a Harry Potter backpack for a million dollars, but Kassie treasures her Harry Potter imagination. As is typical of gifted children her age, Kassie has an advanced vocabulary, precocious reading skills, and an uncanny ability to turn words to images, images to symbols, and symbols to personal reality. She doesn't need an insignia on a backpack, a commercial chocolate frog, or any other "real" objects to get her going; she constructs her reality from the unreal, and she does it rather well.

Bettelheim (1976) explained that a child recognizes that stories are told "in the language of symbols and not that of everyday reality" (p. 73), that fantasy is not an accurate portrayal or *specific* guide to dealing with everyday life. As Bettelheim expressed it, "Although [fantasy] stories are *unreal*, they are not *untrue*" (p. 73), as they reflect not external reality, but "inner processes taking place in the individual" (p. 25). Indeed, T. A. Barron (2001), an author of successful fantasies, has claimed that "paradoxical as it sounds, the best fantasy is true. It must be—to win our honest belief in a brand-new world with brand-new rules" (p. 53).

Particularly for a gifted child who is inclined to explore abstractions, test generalizations, and explore what is often termed the "highest levels of human thought" (Frazier, 1982, as cited in Jeon, 1992), this process occurs naturally. Speaking of brand-new rules, Quidditch provides a simple, clear example of this process. The game of Quidditch involves a set of implements, a cast of players, and a complex set of rules and strategies far different from any game a reader such as Kassie has ever seen. (Indeed, it would take a child as gifted as Kassie to visualize it.) But, beyond the broomsticks and silver snitches, Kassie and children like her can see something familiar: The behavior of the competing players and their friends—not to mention some of their professors—is true to human nature, and a child with gifted sensitivities can see the inhabitants of her school and neighborhood peeking from beneath the wizard robes. A gifted reader notices Harry, who has spent the first 11 years of his life in a cupboard under the stairs, beginning to develop self-efficacy as he becomes aware of his talent and actualizes the skills he needs to achieve the victory that comes to mean so much to him.

Kassie does not consider herself an athlete, and she is not particularly interested in basketball, the game that author J. K. Rowling has said is the closest existing game to Quidditch (Schafer, 2000). But, as a violin student, Kassie is finding some of those student concertos to be about as challenging as chasing a snitch. To a gifted child like Kassie, Quidditch isn't about handling balls: It's about handling talent, desire, work, accomplishment, peer relationships, competition, and performance psychology.

A child with Kassie's innate responsiveness to symbols would accept a writing (or even a conversational) prompt with about as much enthusiasm as she'd give to the decorated backpack. Kassie's mother, a teacher education professor, has read the Harry Potter books (during Kassie's first time through), but she knows enough to step back and let Kassie construct her own meaning. As Bettelheim (1976) advised, adult coaching denies the child the opportunity to cope personally with the problems portrayed in the story. As the child brings imagination, intellect, and emotions together in identifying with the characters, "inner resources" develop that enable the child to cope with "the vagaries of life" (p. 4). The child thus gains "confidence in himself [or herself] and in his [or her] future" (p. 4). Perhaps after reading about the sorting hat that sits atop the head of each new student, assesses the neophyte's strengths and weaknesses, and places the student in the proper "house" (sort of a cross between a dorm and a fraternity), a parent or a teacher could venture a question about how or why people are constantly sorting and classifying each other. But, with a child like Kassie, it should be only a question. A process drama might be based around the mirror of Erised, in which the viewer sees him- or herself experiencing his or her deepest desire, but participants would need to choose their own personas (themselves or a "safer" one) and improvise in whatever direction they prefer. A teacher should furnish only the mirror.

The Uses of Identification

Throughout her life, Sally has had ambivalent feelings about talents that made her different from other children her age. At age 7, she was criticized by her second-grade teacher who caught her reading Shakespeare's *As You Like It*, though her fifth-grade teacher read *Les Misérables* along with Sally so she could discuss it with her. At 8, Sally was mocked by neighborhood children when they heard her practicing her violin, but at 10 she enjoyed the attention she got from participating in a weekly university master class. At one point, she started learning Russian so she could someday study at the Moscow Conservatory, while at another time she yelled out her refusal to play anything very difficult in public: "I'm not going to be anybody's wow child!" Like many gifted children, Sally fought against expectations—her own and those of others—which pulled her in many directions at once.

Among the issues listed by VanTassel-Baska (1983) that are involved in coping with giftedness are some that Sally shares with Harry Potter: (a) comprehending "one's differentness," (b) developing tolerance for others and for oneself, and (c) gaining a perception of one's unique complement of weaknesses and strengths (cited by Jeon, 1992).

Gifted children may see their own conflicts in the talented young wizards at Hogwarts. When a jealous Draco taunts Harry, Sally may recall the neighbor child who sent nasty notes when she received attention for performing. When Harry's best friend Ron overcomes his jealousy to support Harry in his quest for the Wizard Cup, Sally may recall her adolescent self-hugging and encouraging a friend who was stepping onto the stage to perform a concerto—an honor for which Sally had auditioned and lost. When Harry cringes as Gilderoy Lockhart pulls him up to pose for photographers, Sally can remember the times that attention, praise, and publicity embarrassed her. Gifted children see so many of the challenges and conflicts of giftedness played out in the Harry Potter books, and they naturally identify and respond.

In analyzing the use of books in helping gifted children deal with their needs and problems, Jeon (1992) noted that using their imagination allows children to experiment with different approaches to problems without the consequences that might follow in a real-life situation. Fantasy author Susan Cooper (1990) referred to this as "amazing adventures with no price tag" (p. 309).

For both a young child like Maria who identifies with characters on a fairly concrete level and an older student like Sally who looks at more abstract, less obvious connections, journals are a way to draw out and examine those parallels and relationships. Children Maria's age—either individually, as a special-interest group, or as a full class—can write a simulated journal pretending to be Harry Potter, recording what happens to him and how he feels about people and events. Similar to art therapy or play therapy, this expression enables children to portray feelings in symbolic form without the price tag that blunt expression often brings.

In *Harry Potter and the Chamber of Secrets*, Tom Riddle, a former student at Hogwarts who later became the evil Lord Voldemort, has preserved his youthful self in the pages of a diary. As everything at Hogwarts, including diaries, is magical, Tom can continue to communicate through the diary and almost succeeds in bringing this vigorous young self to life, even though the current Voldemort is feeble and helpless. A gifted upper-elementary student like Kassie or even a young adult like Sally who is seeking to understand her own identity and potential might find interesting symbols in the living journal. How do we preserve ourselves in what we write? How accurately can we portray ourselves? How do we choose what we will preserve? What power lies in these recorded fragments of memory? What and how do they communicate to those who may be yet unborn? Are there ways in which we may actually come back to affect the future through our writing? As they examine their own journals, young people who struggle with their identity may be prompted to seek clues and write for understanding.

Winifred Radigan (2001), a New York City school administrator, has spoken for Kassie, Sally, and a host of other gifted youth:

> What speaks to me is how the books console that inner child who still longs for her magic to be discovered and nurtured; the child within remembers all the times she stood on the outside of the inner circle. Like Hermione, constantly reading and prone to speaking the unpalatable truth, she was avoided until needed for help with homework. Like Harry, she felt that something was wrong with her, that she didn't belong. Like Ron, she didn't have the money for sleek, new toys of the moment or the current style. Like Nigel, she was clumsy at sports and timid. "Surely, surely," she whispered, "I must be a wizard." (p. 694)

Maria, Kassie, and Sally are all looking for their wizard robes, though these robes will be of different sizes and colors.

Does it help the gifted individual to put on the robes, seize a journal, and feel his or her way around the shifting staircases and haunted common rooms of Hogwarts? Bettelheim (1976) wrote of "inner resources," that mutually enriching blend of imagination, emotion, and intellect that keeps an individual from being "at the mercy of the vagaries of life" (p. 4). It is commonly acknowledged that journal writing aids the individual in accomplishing this integration. With the varying gifts represented in their main characters—particularly in Harry and Hermione—the Harry Potter books offer plenty of opportunity to incorporate this experience.

The Uses of Good and Evil

Kassie is not as eager to spend most of her life among her peers as many children her age. She has friends, but she likes to spend some of her time mentoring younger children and conversing with adults, rather than constantly playing with her age-mates. When asked why, Kassie replies that many children her age "do not choose the right." She is particularly upset when she sees her peers "playing with some, but not others." Like most gifted children, Kassie has a lively sense of what is right and what is wrong, and she hates to see anyone's feelings hurt.

Sally, too, has had from a very young age strong sensitivities relating to justice, equity, fairness, human suffering, and human worth. As a child, she suffered teasing and exclusion on the playground because she did not return the ringleader's taunting or manipulation. As a teen, her arms were the refuge for abused or even suicidal friends. As a young adult, she sang "I am a child of God" with neglected children on the streets of London.

Gifted individuals have a drive to make sense of lives beyond their own. Bettelheim (1976) cited J. R. R. Tolkien's statement that what matters most to the child who reads fantasy is not "Is it true?," but rather addressing the main character, "Was he good?" or "Was he wicked?" (p. 117). The Harry Potter books have been denounced by some parents and religious groups because they portray evil with dark symbolism that some fear will be frightening to children. Similar charges have been leveled through the years against fairy tales such as "Snow

White" and "Hansel and Gretel" and, more recently, against such fantasies as C. S. Lewis' *The Chronicles of Narnia* and J. R. R. Tolkien's *The Lord of the Rings.*

Bettelheim (1976) answered such critics with the comment that a story that shows only the sunny aspects of life "nourishes the mind only in a one-sided way, and real life is not all sunny" (p. 7). Fairy tales, he affirmed (and, by generalization, other forms of light/dark fantasy), bring children face to face with the basic predicaments of humankind. Children encounter adversity and struggle, but realize that the main character cannot achieve his or her true identity without meeting such difficulties and overcoming them. And, when the hero seems about to be overcome, "benevolent powers [a fairy godmother, a woodsman, or a sorting hat and a phoenix named Fawkes] will come to his aid, and he will succeed" (p. 24). Bettelheim explained that, as children identify, struggle, and suffer and triumph with the hero, the "imprint" of the hero's morality transfers to them. Rather than feeling discouraged over the hero's suffering, children are energized by his or her victory (Pierce, 1993, p. 51).

Joseph Campbell's (1968) influential work *The Hero With a Thousand Faces* compares the heroes of world mythology, folklore, and fairy tales in order "to uncover some of the truths disguised for us under the figures of religion and mythology" (p. vii). He claims that "the parallels . . . will develop a vast and amazingly constant statement of the basic truths by which man has lived throughout the millenniums of his residence on the planet" (p. vii). Many gifted children have a natural affinity for comparisons, contrasts, and interrelationships, along with a natural fascination with heroes. Thus, comparing the "hero's journey" of Harry Potter to that of a variety of heroes throughout the ages would be simultaneously a fascination and a challenge.

On the surface, perhaps a bespectacled, tousle-headed, lightning-scarred kid who spends the first part of his life living in a cupboard under the stairs and most of his teenage years in a castle-school for young witches and wizards has little in common with Hercules, Siegfried, Maui, and other heroes who beckon from the pages of folklore, mythology, and classic fantasy. But, with the ingenuity characteristic of a gifted child or adolescent, parallels are not difficult to find. According to Campbell (1968),

In sum: the child of destiny has to face a long period of obscurity. This is a time of extreme danger, impediment, or disgrace. He is thrown inward to his own depths or outward to the unknown; either way, what he touches is a darkness unexplored. And this is a zone of unsuspected presences, benign as well as malignant: an angel appears, a helpful animal, a fisherman, a hunter, crone or peasant. Fostered in the animal school, or, like Siegfried, below ground among the gnomes that nourish the roots of the tree of life, or again, alone in some little room (the story has been told a thousand ways), the young world-apprentice learns the lesson of the seed powers, which reside just beyond the sphere of the measured and the named. (pp. 326–327)

Certainly Harry, the despised child raised by hostile relatives, begins in a state of obscurity, and his selfish and occasionally violent uncle, Vernon Dursley, provides all of the danger and disgrace Campbell might have had in mind. The bumbling half-giant Hagrid is no angel, but he is definitely adequate to get Harry to the school that will enable him to discover and develop his natural gifts.

Campbell (1968) concluded that the challenge of creating a hero in the modern world is "nothing if not that of rendering the modern world spiritually significant . . . nothing if not that of making it possible for men and women to come to full human maturity through the conditions of contemporary life" (p. 388). Harry Potter, the lonely, neglected kid on Privet Drive, is perhaps an unlikely hero, but it is this very unlikeliness that allows him to function as a set of modern symbols for the processes and truths that have been represented by hero and journey symbols through the ages. Gifted children can find these parallels and respond in a variety of literary, artistic, and dramatic formats. As the hero (even Harry) matures, gifted children or adolescents mature, as well. And, as Harry learns to discern and operate between powerful good, personified by Dumbledore, and powerful evil, given form by Voldemort, gifted individuals are able to develop that drive to deal with morality and ethics that seems to be innate within their makeup.

Tamora Pierce (1993), a current author of children's fantasy, referred to fantasy as "the great equalizer between the powerful and the powerless" (p. 51). She recalled early struggles in her own life:

> I visited Tolkien's Mordor often for years, not because I *liked* what went on there, but because on that dead horizon, and then throughout the sky overhead, I could see the interplay and the lasting power of light and hope. It got me through. (p. 51)

Pierce concluded, "Fantasy creates hope and optimism in readers. It is the pure stuff of wonder, the kind that carries over into everyday life and colors the way readers perceive things around them" (p. 51). Maria, Kassie, and Sally are looking for wonder and optimism in a world threatened by violence, corruption, mass weaponry, and war. They need all the heroes, light, and hope they can get.

Conclusion

Another year at Hogwarts has come to an end. Voldemort has been overcome (though not destroyed); mysteries have been unraveled; injuries have healed; friendships have been tested, but have endured; Harry, Ron, and Hermione have faced a variety of trials and broken a few rules, but have emerged a little stronger and a little wiser.

Though circumstances of the plots have varied widely, according to J. K. Rowling's wonderful imagination, each book ends in much the same way—the classic way of fantasy. The hero has entered the fantasy world, faced dangers, struggled with trials, experienced victories and setbacks, overcome the evil or dark force, and eventually reentered the real world. Now, he is able to cope better with the challenges life offers.

To accomplish his journey of development and renewal, Harry Potter and his friends are transported to a place where they learn to maximize and control the magic powers within them. Can a gifted child who is sensing unusual powers within him- or herself find answers and understanding in a place as far-away magical as Hogwarts or in a child who uses magic words, magic potions, and magic wands to attack his difficulties? According to Bettelheim (1976), "Every child believes in magic" (p. 118). Bettelheim wrote that he had seen in his psychiatric practice children who had never been introduced to fantasy literature who had "invested an electric fan or motor with as much magic and destructive power" (p. 118) as the wildest and wickedest of fantasy characters. Children—especially gifted children with their vivid imaginations, their need to understand their own humanity and differences, and their heightened concern for ethics and morality—can find in fantasy a magical place where it is reasonably safe to act out the conflicts they face in growing up and encountering the world.

Those who know the genre best, fantasy writers, express the magic of their tales:

Imagination

Once the child's imagination is caught up in that book, particularly if it deals with experiences beyond his own world, beyond reality—then boundaries vanish, walls disappear, and he finds himself facing a wonderful space in which anything can happen. He's transported into [a] dream theater.

—Susan Cooper, author of the series
The Dark is Rising. (1990, p. 305)

Identification

Emotional truth goes beyond the senses, engaging our hearts. In compelling tales of fantasy, we believe the emotional elements as fully as if they had happened during our own lives.

—T. A. Barron, author of the series The Lost Years of Merlin
(2001, p. 54)

Good and Evil

A fleeting glimpse of Joy, Joy beyond the walls of the world.

—J. R. R. Tolkien, author
of the series The Lord of the Rings (1989)

There is much that we need to give our gifted children, and pressing is the need to guide them to gifts that they can give themselves. Lewis Carroll, who many consider to be the leader of the development of fantasy as a form of literature for children, has given us a hint in his tender designation: "the love-gift of a fairy tale" (as quoted in Bettelheim, 1976).

References

Barron, T. A. (2001). Truth and dragons. *School Library Journal, 47,* 52–54.

Bettelheim, B. (1976). *The uses of enchantment: The meaning and importance of fairy tales.* New York: Knopf.

Campbell, J. (1968). *The hero with a thousand faces* (2nd ed.). Princeton, NJ: Princeton University Press.

Cooper, S. (1990). Fantasy in the real world. *The Horn Book, 66,* 304–314.

Gooderham, D. (1995). Children's fantasy literature: Toward an anatomy. *Children's Literature in Education, 26*(3), 171–182.

Jeon, K. W. (1992). Bibliotherapy for gifted children. *Gifted Child Today, 15*(6), 16–19.

Pierce, T. (1993). Fantasy: Why kids read it, why kids need it. *School Library Journal, 39*(10), 50–51.

Radigan, W. M. (2001). Connecting the generations: Memory, magic, and Harry Potter. *Journal of Adolescent and Adult Literacy, 44*(8), 694.

Rowling, J. K. (1998). *Harry Potter and the sorcerer's stone.* New York: Scholastic.

Rowling, J. K. (1999). *Harry Potter and the chamber of secrets.* New York: Scholastic.

Rowling, J. K. (1999). *Harry Potter and the prisoner of Azkaban.* New York: Scholastic.

Rowling, J. K. (2000). *Harry Potter and the goblet of fire.* New York: Scholastic.

Schafer, E. (2000). *Exploring Harry Potter.* Osprey, FL: Beacham.

Tolkien, J. R. R. (1989). *Tree and leaf.* Boston: Houghton-Mifflin.

chapter 2

Gifted Kids, Gifted Characters, and Great Books

by **Bertie Kingore**

gifted 10-year-old reacted to E. L. Konigsburg's female protagonist in *From the Mixed-Up Files of Mrs. Basil E. Frankweiler* (1967) by exclaiming, "Claudia is so much like me! She's so bright, she uses logic and plans, but most of all, she wants to do something important with her life. That's exactly how I feel. I don't want my life to just be regular."

Quality literature involving gifted characters should be available to gifted children and adolescents to encourage reflection about their feelings, concerns, and interests. These books can help students gain insights into their own lives and identify with others. Librarians know that children frequently seek books about "kids like me." However, because the development of key characters who are gifted is not typical in most books, children need help in locating those with such characters.

The annotated bibliography in this chapter focuses on the following three criteria: (1) the books are written by authors of merit; (2) each book contains well-developed characters who display gifted behaviors; and (3) the stories include thought-provoking problem situations, issues, or personal needs with which gifted students can identify. These titles are widely available in libraries and many bookstores. A few of them may be temporarily out of print, as publishers are seasonal in their reprinting. However, they are well-worth looking for in your library or may be ordered from interlibrary loan.

You can locate additional titles relating to specific social and emotional needs in *The Best of Bookfinder: A Guide to Children's Literature About Interests and Concerns of Youth Aged 2–18* (Spredemann-Dreyer, 1992). While most books listed in that resource do not involve gifted characters, the annotated bibliographies may still prove useful for individual needs.

Since it prompts opinions and emotional reactions, another source certain to motivate gifted students is the article "One Hundred Books That Shaped the Century" (Breen, Fader, Odean, & Sutherland, 2000), in which a team of experts selected the 20th century's most significant books for children and young adults. Many gifted readers will be intrigued to find out how many recognized books they have read and debate with others why certain cherished books that didn't make the list should have.

The books listed in this chapter exemplify multiple kinds of giftedness, including academic/intellectual, performing arts, creativity, specific subject areas, leadership, and psychomotor. It is significant that the characters displaying giftedness in these books represent diverse ethnic populations and a broad span of socioeconomic levels. Thus, these characters model how gifted potentials exist and require nurturing in every population.

The books incorporate a wide range of gifted characteristics through the behaviors and needs of the characters. Different characters in these stories demonstrate combinations of advanced language, complex analyzing and problem solving, content depth and expertise, unique points of view, sensitivity, and a sophisticated sense of humor (Kingore, 2001). Many of the characters use their advanced potentials to benefit others. In *Sara Crewe* (Burnet, 1981), the main character notes that "a person who was clever ought to be clever enough not to be unjust or deliberately unkind to any one . . . so she would be as polite as she could to people who in the least deserved politeness" (p. 28).

Be alert, however, that giftedness is not always portrayed in a positive light; some gifted characters, like other humans, display negative qualities. In *Matilda* (Dahl, 1988) for example, Roald Dahl develops comic relief by posturing the parents as selfish dolts and having the main character use her intellectual genius to get back at some adults as she tries to help her nice teacher, Miss Honey.

Two listed books have animals instead of human characters, and they are worth mentioning for the gifted characteristics they exemplify and the messages they model. Bright young children enjoy identifying with these fantasy figures. Sylvester, in *Sylvester and the Magic Pebble* (Steig, 1969), unassumingly uses an advanced vocabulary, and his sensitivity reminds us that love is more important in life than material possessions. The eponymous protagonist in *Frederick* (Lionni, 1967) documents the significant value of imagination and creativity by suggesting that psychological truth exists in our dreams and that it helps sustain us in difficult times.

The genre of biographies deserves special consideration as being highly applicable for gifted learners. Biographies and autobiographies frequently serve as role models for gifted students by illustrating how even prominent or successful people experience triumphs, failures, and hardships throughout their lives. Encourage gifted students to seek biographies of famous people in their areas of interests. Librarians can recommend numerous biographies or books with biographic vignettes relating to specific content areas. For example, the bibliography in this chapter includes Bedard's (1992) *Emily* (writing); Krull's (1996) *Wilma Unlimited: How Wilma Rudolph Became the World's Fastest Woman* (athletics); Roberts' (1986) *Henry Cisneros: Mexican American Mayor* (politics); Parks and Haskins' (1992) *Rosa Parks: My Story* (civil action); Freedman's (1991) *The Wright Brothers: How They Invented the Airplane* (aviation); and Martin's (1998) *Snowflake Bentley* (science and photography).

Parents and teachers should read a book first before suggesting it to a student. By reading the book yourself, you may increase your own insight into giftedness, be better prepared to discuss the book with the child, and avoid recommending a book that is not appropriate for a particular individual. Obviously, you should make selected books accessible to children, rather than force books upon them. After a child has read a book, be available not only to discuss it, but more importantly, to listen to the student's perceptions. When appropriate, encourage children to talk about areas of the book in which they agreed or disagreed with the character's actions and encourage them to pose alternative problem approaches and solutions.

Suggested age levels are based on the ages of the gifted characters, the complexity of the issues confronting them, and the interest or appeal to gifted readers. However, since gifted learners frequently read and comprehend advanced materials, adults who know the child can only determine the appropriate levels of materials.

Annotated Bibliography

Avi. (1991). *Nothing but the truth: A documentary novel.* New York: Orchard Books.
Avi's book emerges as a witty satire of high school politics that invites the reader to question and analyze what they read and hear from the mass media. (Grades 4–8)

Bedard, M. (1992). *Emily.* New York: Doubleday.
An insightful vignette of the reclusive life of Emily Dickinson is shared through a young neighbor's visit. (Grades 3–6)

Burnett, F. H. (1981). *Sara Crewe.* New York: Putnam.
Although the book was originally written in 1888, the eponymous protagonist remains courageous and compassionate as she is orphaned and falls from riches to a pauper. (Grades 2–6)

Curtis, C. P. (1999). *Bud, not Buddy.* New York: Delacorte.
This well-crafted novel explores the life and hard times of a resourceful orphan in search of his father during the Great Depression. (Grades 4–8)

Dahl, R. (1988). *Matilda.* New York: Viking.
Matilda, a genius with selfish dolts for parents, uses her untapped mental ability to punish some hurtful adults and save her nice teacher. (Grades 2–6)

Fitzgerald, J. D. (1967). *The Great Brain.* New York: Dial.
This is the first title of an extensive series exploring the adventures of a genius main character. (Grades 2–6)

Fitzhugh, L. (1964). *Harriet, the spy.* New York: Harper & Row.
Harriet is intelligent and curious. She writes observations of her neighbors and classmates and then must devise a creative solution to convince her friends to forgive her. (Grades 1–5)

Fox, M. (1985). *Wilford Gordon McDonald Partridge.* New York: Kane/Miller.
Wilford's favorite friend at the retirement home loses her memory, and he wants to figure out how to find it for her. (Grades K–3)

Freedman, R. (1991). *The Wright Brothers: How they invented the airplane.* New York: Scholastic.
This nonfiction book uses historical photographs and in-depth information to explain the determination and creativity leading to Wilber and Orville Wright's invention of the airplane. (Grades 4–8)

George, J. C. (1959). *My side of the mountain.* New York: Dutton.
Sam's diary reveals his experiences living alone and off the land in the Catskill Mountains. (Grades 3–6)

Hamilton, V. (1971). *The planet of Junior Brown.* New York: Macmillan.
Junior Brown is a talented pianist whose weight causes people to ostracize him. This inner-city story weaves a complex tale about friendship, loyalty, and learning to live together. (Grades 5–8)

Hoffman, M. (1991). *Amazing Grace.* New York: Dial Books.
When Grace wants to try out for the role of Peter Pan, her family encourages her to be what she wants to be, but her friends are not as supportive. (Grades K–3)

Konigsburg, E. L. (1967). *From the mixed-up files of Mrs. Basil E. Frankweiler.* New York: Atheneum.
A sister and a brother run away from home to hide in the

Metropolitan Museum of Art in New York City and decipher the mystery of a statue. (Grades 3–7)

Konigsburg, E. L. (1996). *The view from Saturday.* New York: Scholastic.
Four gifted students and their teacher form a team for the Academic Bowl and enhance their humanity in the process. (Grades 4–8)

Krull, K. (1996). *Wilma unlimited: How Wilma Rudolph became the world's fastest woman.* San Diego, CA: Harcourt Brace.
This is a simple, but informative biography of Wilma Rudolph overcoming polio, struggling to walk, and finally becoming an Olympic runner. (Grades 2–6)

L'Engle, M. (1962). *A wrinkle in time.* New York: Farrar, Straus, & Giroux;
L'Engle, M. (1973). *A wind in the door.* New York: Farrar, Straus, & Giroux. (Sequel)
L'Engle, M. (1978). *A swiftly tilting planet.* New York: Farrar, Straus & Giroux. (Sequel)
The family members in this classic science-fiction trilogy travel the cosmos, face the problem of being different, fight to overcome evil, and discover the power of love. (Grades 3–8)

Levine, G. C. (1997). *Ella enchanted.* New York: Harper Collins.
In this Cinderella-based novel, the spunky, intelligent heroine struggles to overcome the curse that forces her to obey any command given to her. (Grades 3–8)

Lionni, L. (1967). *Frederick.* New York: Random House.
Frederick is different, and the other mice have to learn to appreciate him and his talents. (Grades K–3)

Lowry, L. (1993). *The giver.* New York: Bantam Doubleday Dell.
This complex novel relates the story of a perfect world with no problems, fears, or pain. *The Giver* holds the memories of the pain and pleasure of life for the rest of the population. (Grades 4–8)

MacLachlan, P. (1988). *The facts and fictions of Minna Pratt.* New York: Harper & Row.
Minna is a talented musician who struggles to learn to appreciate herself and the uniqueness of her family. (Grades 4–8)

Martin, J. B. (1998). *Snowflake Bentley.* Boston: Houghton-Mifflin.
Persistence and family support are taught in this biography of Wilson "Snowflake" Bentley, a self-taught photographer and scientist. (Grades 2–6)

Parks, R., & Haskins, J. (1992). *Rosa Parks: My story.* New York: Penguin.
Rosa Parks tells her story, including the famous incident on the Montgomery bus. (Grades K–5)

Paterson, K. (1977). *Bridge to Terabithia.* New York: Avon.
Two nonconformist friends create their own magical realm and encourage each other's gifts as they grow in self-discovery. (Grades 4–8)

Paterson, K. (1985). *Come sing, Jimmy Jo.* New York: Dutton.
Painful shyness causes self and family conflicts for a gifted 11-year-old boy when he reluctantly joins his family's musical group. (Grades 4–8)

Paterson, K. (1980). *Jacob have I loved.* New York: Avon.
Complex relationships and emotions evolve as a twin feels that her sister has deprived her of parental affection and schooling. (Grades 6–8)

Paulsen, G. (1996). *Brian's winter.* New York: Scholastic
When the plane crashes, Brian is the sole survivor and must solve unique survival problems. (Grades 3–8)

Raskin, E. (1978). *The westing game.* New York: Avon.
This mystery challenges the reader to follow 16 characters and plotline twists to solve a puzzle. (Grades 3–8)

Roberts, M. (1986). *Henry Cisneros: Mexican American Mayor.* Chicago: Children's Press.
This is the biography of the national government official and former mayor of San Antonio, Texas. (Grades 3–8)

Ross, T. (1994). *Eggbert the slightly cracked egg.* New York: G. P. Putnam's Sons.
With a generous serving of puns, Eggbert uses his creativity and has many adventures trying to fit in and be accepted. (Grades K–2)

Sobol, D. J. (1963). *Encyclopedia Brown: Boy detective.* New York: Thomas Nelson.
The first title of an extensive series of mysteries that the hero must solve. (Grades 1–4)

Steig, W. (1969). *Sylvester and the magic pebble.* New York: Prentice Hall.
Sylvester is in a predicament when he finds a magic stone and a hungry lion. This is a perfect story for illustrating loving family relationships and modeling sophisticated vocabulary. (Grades K–4)

Taylor, M. (1976). *Roll of thunder, hear my cry.* New York: Dial Books
Taylor, M. (1981). *Let the circle Be unbroken.* New York: Dial Books. (Sequel)
Cassie and her brother, children of a Black schoolteacher, face subtle and explicit racial prejudice in the early 20th century. (Grades 3–8)

Voight, C. (1981). *The homecoming.* New York: Atheneum.
Voight, C. (1982). *Dicey's song.* New York: Atheneum. (Prequel)
With determination and creative problem solving, a young girl struggles to keep her family together after their mother abandons them. (Grades 3–8)

Wynne-Jones, T. (1995). *The maestro.* New York: Orchard Books.
Burl's life is changed in one day when he runs away from his

abusive father and stumbles upon an eccentric genius living in a remote cabin. (Grades 4–8)

References

Breen, K., Fader E., Odean, K., & Sutherland, Z. (2000, January). One hundred books that shaped the century. *School Library Journal,* 50–58.

Kingore, B. (2001). *The Kingore observation inventory* (*KOI*; 2nd ed). Austin, TX: Professional Associates.

Spredemann-Dreyer, S. (Ed.). (1992). *The best of Bookfinder: A guide to children's literature about interests and concerns of youth aged 2–18.* Circle Pines, MN: American Guidance Service.

chapter 3

Using Multicultural Literature in Gifted Education Classrooms

by **Donna Y. Ford, Tyrone C. Howard,**
  and **J. John Harris III**

*t*oday's classrooms are very different from class-rooms of a decade ago. Today, teachers work in classrooms of unparalleled diversity. Students differ in terms of ability, race or ethnicity, socioeconomic status (SES), and many other variables. Thus, teachers are constantly searching for instructional strategies and curricula to meet diverse cognitive, academic, and affective needs.

The search for materials and strategies to challenge gifted students will often lead to the works of Joyce VanTassel-Baska, June Maker, Carol Tomlinson, Joseph Renzulli, Benjamin Bloom, and others who have created guidelines, strategies, and materials that target the cognitive and academic needs of gifted students. Similarly, teachers can rely on the works of Banks (1994), Grant and Sleeter (1998), and other multicultural educators when seeking materials and strategies that meet the needs of racially and culturally diverse students.

However, when searching for resources to understand and meet the needs of students who are gifted *and* minority, teachers may be less successful.

Likewise, it is difficult to find multicultural materials that challenge advanced learners, regardless of race or culture. This chapter addresses this void by presenting a framework (based upon *Multicultural Gifted Education*, Ford & Harris, 1999; the actual model is called the "Ford-Harris Matrix") that teachers can use to create a curriculum that

1. challenges gifted students because it promotes critical thinking;
2. meets the needs of minority students because it is multicultural; and
3. exposes White students to quality multicultural literature and important multicultural concepts and issues.

The first goal is addressed using Bloom's (1956) cognitive taxonomy, while the last two goals are addressed using Banks' (1994) multicultural education model. In the following sections, we present a rationale for infusing multicultural education into school curricula, briefly review Bloom's cognitive taxonomy, and explain Banks' multicultural model. Finally, we present a literature-based lesson using the framework presented in this chapter and elsewhere (Ford & Harris, 1999). Our motive in writing this chapter and creating the framework is simple: We are targeting the question "How can educators create curricula and learning experiences that promote higher levels of thinking *and* higher levels of multicultural learning?"

Multicultural Education: An Overview

The title of *Learning in Living Color* (Valdez, 1999) succinctly reflects the racial demography of classrooms in many school districts. In virtually every school building, one is likely to find students of color, and this diversity is increasing each day. Therefore, teachers in contemporary classrooms must reexamine their curricula and instructional strategies to meet the needs of these students. For example, Shade, Kelly, and Oberg (1997), Ladson-Billings (1990), and many other minority scholars have called upon educators to create "culturally responsive" classrooms that help students understand and negotiate differences across cultures. Teachers in culturally responsive classrooms emphasize that students can *learn* to become pluralistic in their thought, behavior, and affect. Teachers ask questions, for example, that promote higher level thinking about multicultural topics, concepts, issues, and groups, and they create learning experiences that promote cultural empathy.

Multicultural Education Goals

Multicultural education has several goals. It endeavors to ground students with multicultural knowledge, to adopt educational equity and cultural pluralism as philosophies, to empower students and promote student social action, and to teach from a multicultural perspective.

1. *Multicultural knowledge* increases students' sense of self-worth and belief that they have a chance for a successful future. Multicultural knowledge lays the foundation for developing cultural pluralism, intergroup harmony, and the ability to think, work, and live with a multicultural perspective.

2. *Educational equity* has three fundamental conditions: (a) an equal opportunity to learn; (b) positive educational outcomes for both individuals and groups; and (c) equal physical and financial conditions for students to grow to their fullest potential cognitively, academically, and affectively.

3. Working with *cultural pluralism* in mind, educators modify fundamental educational conditions to promote equitable learning. When school personnel support cultural pluralism, they ask themselves the important question: How can I help my students develop understanding, respect, and appreciation for individuals who are culturally different from themselves?

4. *Empowerment* helps students become independent and interdependent learners. Empowerment connotes social action; it helps students take an active role in improving the quality of their (and other) communities.

5. *Social action* promotes intergroup and intragroup harmony. Thus, educators provide knowledge, skills, and a classroom environment that prepare students to live and work with members of their own cultural groups and members of other cultural groups. Instruction includes opportunities for students to work together, to learn from each other, and to rely on each other.

6. *Teaching with a multicultural perspective* means that teachers see that culture, race, gender, religion, SES, and ability are powerful variables in the learning process and that important ideas about teaching can be gained from studying cultural systems. When teaching from a multicultural perspective, educators challenge assumptions and stereotypes; they examine curricula from a broader point of view and in an assertive, proactive manner. Essentially, educators endeavor to promote cultural continuity between the home and school of minority students and attempt to eliminate culturally assaultive classrooms.

Infusing Multicultural Content Into Gifted Education

One of the most prolific scholars in multicultural education is James Banks. Banks' model presents four levels of ways to integrate multicultural content into the curriculum (see Figure 3.1). These levels rely heavily on one's philosophy about and experiences with multicultural education. For example, at the lowest two levels, teachers may have little preparation in multicultural education; hence, they are unable to teach at higher levels. Further, teachers who do not hold strong values about multicultural education may, if focusing on a multicultural concept or topic, choose to work at the lowest levels.

At the lowest level, the *Contributions Approach*, educators focus on heroes, holidays, and discrete elements. This is the most frequently adopted and extensively used approach to multiculturalism in the schools, yet it is the most simplistic. In this approach, the traditional ethnocentric curriculum remains unchanged in its basic structure, goals, and salient characteristics. Frequently, cultural traditions, foods, music, and dance

Social Action Level (4)

Students identify important social problems and issues, gather pertinent data, clarify their values on the issues, make decisions, and take reflective actions to help resolve the issue or problem. Students seek to make a social and cultural difference. They are able to apply and synthesize their learning.

Transformation Level (3)

The basic goals, structure, and nature of the curriculum are changed to enable students to view concepts, events, issues, problems, and themes from the perspectives of diverse groups. Students are prepared cognitively and affectively (emotionally) to work with complex and important multicultural concepts, events, etc.

Additive Level (2)

Consists of additions to the content, concepts, themes, and perspectives to the curriculum without changing its structure. Because students are not exposed to substantive and controversial multicultural concepts, they are not cognitively or affectively (emotionally) prepared to understanding what is taught.

Contributions Level (1)

Heroes, cultural components, holidays, and other discrete elements related to ethnic groups are added to the curriculum on special days, occasions, and celebrations. This is the most basic and rudimentary level. It is least effective and may promote and/or increase stereotypes and misinformation.

**Figure 3.1. Banks' Model on Levels
of Infusing Multicultural Content Into Curriculum**

may be discussed, but little or no attention is given to their meaning and significance to minority groups. Although ethnic content is limited primarily to special days, weeks, and months related to minority groups, students learn little to nothing about the occasion, group, or individuals being "celebrated." The Contributions Approach is cosmetic; it provides teachers with a quick, nonthreatening way to "integrate" the curriculum, and teachers can adopt this approach without knowing much about racially and culturally diverse groups. It often reinforces stereotypes about minority groups, while using safe, nonthreatening heroes found acceptable to the mainstream.

In the second level, the *Additive Approach*, the content, concepts, themes, and perspectives of minority groups are added to the curriculum, but without being integrated throughout the curriculum. Thus, the basic curricular structure remains unchanged. For instance, teachers may add a multicultural book or unit to one particular course, but not to another. This piecemeal approach does not help students understand multicultural concepts, issues, and groups in a coherent or systematic way. That is, while the content changes slightly, there is little restructuring of the curriculum relative to purposes and characteristics. Minority students still learn little of their own history, and White students learn little of the history and contributions of other racial and cultural groups to American society. This approach requires little time, effort, training, and rethinking of curriculum and instruction.

The third level is the *Transformational Approach*. At this level, two transformations occur. First, the structure of the curriculum changes so students are given opportunities to view concepts, issues, events, and themes from the perspectives of minority groups. Second, there are changes relative to the fundamental assumptions, goals, nature, and structure of the curriculum. These two transformations provide students with a critical awareness of, understanding of, and respect for multicultural concepts, events, and people.

The *Social Action Approach* is the highest level. Here, students make decisions on important social issues and take action to help solve them. Students are not socialized to accept mainstream ideologies, practices, and institutions. Instead, they feel empowered and are proactive; they participate in social change because they have the knowledge and perspective to do so. Student self-examination becomes central in this level because of attention to value analysis, decision making, problem solving, and social action experiences. For example, students examine issues surrounding prejudice and discrimination and develop ways to improve race relations. This approach is least likely to be adopted by educators primarily because they lack formal training, experience, understanding, and personal knowledge of other racial and cultural groups (e.g., histories, values, beliefs, customs). This approach and the Transformation Approach require substantive preparation, as well as time and commitment.

Developing Multicultural Gifted Education Experiences: A Framework

Elsewhere, we have provided detailed strategies for partnering multicultural education and gifted education (Ford & Harris, 1999). One such strategy is to blend the works of Banks (1994) and Bloom (1956) to create what we call "multicultural gifted education." This framework uses the Ford-Harris Matrix, which is described in Figure 3.2. The framework and matrix are a guide for helping educators (1) promote higher level thinking based on Bloom's cognitive taxonomy (knowledge, comprehension, application, analysis, synthesis, and evaluation) and (2) promote multicultural thinking based on the four levels presented by Banks. Figures 3.1 and 3.2 can help educators develop questions and learning experiences that are challenging, rigorous, and multicultural. Educators are able to monitor the extent to which they are asking questions, providing experiences, and so forth at the higher levels using the models of Bloom and Banks.

Specifically, when teaching at the lowest levels of the Ford-Harris Matrix (i.e., knowledge-contributions, comprehension-contributions, knowledge-additive, comprehension-additive, application-contributions, application-additive), teachers target fact-based questions, statements, and activities that do not promote substantive thinking about multicultural concepts and events. Specifically, at the knowledge-contributions level, students are taught and know facts about cultural artifacts, events, groups, and other cultural elements. At the comprehension-additive level, students are taught and can understand cultural concepts and themes.

Conversely, at the highest levels of the matrix, students think critically about and take action on multicultural topics, concepts, material, and events (i.e., analysis-transformation, analysis-social action, synthesis-transformation, synthesis-social action, evaluation-transformation, and evaluation-social action). It is at these higher levels that educators are able to meet the goals and objectives of multicultural education, as described earlier. Similarly, at these higher levels, gifted students are challenged cognitively—a primary goal of gifted education.

	Knowledge	Comprehension	Application
Contributions	Students are taught and know facts about cultural artifacts, events, groups, and other cultural elements.	Students show an understanding of information about cultural artifacts, groups, etc.	Students are asked to and can apply information learned on cultural artifacts, events, etc.
Additive	Students are taught and know concepts and themes about cultural groups.	Students are taught and can understand cultural concepts and themes.	Students are required to and can apply information learned about cultural concepts and themes.
Transformation	Students are given information on important cultural elements, groups, etc., and can understand this information from different perspectives.	Students are taught to understand and can demonstrate an understanding of important cultural concepts and themes from different perspectives.	Students are asked to and can apply their understanding of important concepts and themes from different perspectives.
Social Action	Based on information on cultural artifacts, etc., students make recommendations for social action.	Based on their understanding of important concepts and themes, students make recommendations for social action.	Students are asked to apply their understanding of important social and cultural issues; they make recommendations for and take action on these issues.

Figure 3.2. **Ford-Harris Matrix of Multi-**

Analysis	Synthesis	Evaluation
Students are taught to and can analyze (e.g., compare and contrast) information about cultural artifacts, groups, etc.	Students are required to and can create a new product from the information on cultural artifacts, groups, etc.	Students are taught to and can evaluate facts and information based on cultural artifacts, groups, etc.
Students are taught to and can analyze important cultural concepts and themes.	Students are asked to and can synthesis important information on cultural concepts and themes.	Students are taught to and can critique cultural concepts and themes.
Students are taught to and can examine important cultural concepts and themes from more than one perspective.	Students are required to and can create a product based on their new perspective or the perspective of another group.	Students are taught to and can evaluate or judge important cultural concepts and themes from different viewpoints (e.g., minority group).
Students are required to and can analyze social and cultural issues from different perspectives; they take action on these issues.	Students create a plan of action to address a social and cultural issue(s); they seek important social change.	Students critique important social and cultural issues, and seek to make national and/or international change.

cultural Gifted Education: Definition of Categories

Applying the Framework Using a Literature-Based Example

One of the most popular multicultural books for grades 2–3 is *Amazing Grace* (Hoffman, 1991). Because of its focus on strong family values and gender and racial equity, it is a timely book, one that can address many objectives. It also meets many of the criteria for high-quality multicultural literature. For instance, people of color are depicted positively and nonstereotypically (in terms of pictures and storyline), it focuses on an important multicultural concept or issue, and the situation is authentic.

In this brief lesson, we first present questions and experiences using Bloom's taxonomy. Next, we present questions and experiences using the Ford-Harris Matrix.

Book Summary

Grace, a Black female, wants to play the part of Peter Pan in a school play, but classmates say that a girl cannot play the role of a boy. Grace is persistent, and with her family's support, she auditions for the part and gets it.

Objectives

Students will focus on important concepts such as persistence and having faith. They will also be introduced to important multicultural concepts such as stereotyping and discrimination. Students will explore and understand the effects of gender and racial stereotyping. They will develop strategies for dealing with situations that are unfair or violates someone's rights.

Only a few objectives have been listed here. However, *Amazing Grace* also lends itself to discussions of strong family values and relationships.

Guiding Questions/Experiences Using Bloom's Cognitive Taxonomy

The following questions and activities are based on Bloom's (1956) cognitive taxonomy. Questions and activities are arranged from the lowest to highest levels:

Knowledge Level
- Who was Peter Pan?
- Who was the main character in the book?
- What did students have to do to get the part of Peter Pan?
- What advice did Grace's mother give her?

Comprehension
- List some positive characteristics about Grace that made it possible for her to play Peter Pan.
- What is the main idea or message of the book?

Application Level
- Write a letter of support to Grace about being persistent.
- Find another book that focuses on persistence and believing in yourself. Tell three ways in which the main character in this book is similar to and different from Grace.
- Find a poem or song that focuses on persistence. Share it with a classmate.

Analysis Level
- How important are effort (working hard) and motivation to success?
- If you were Grace, how would you have handled the peer pressure (e.g., students' comments)?
- Compare *Amazing Grace* to *The Little Engine That Could*. What do they have in common?
- Why is the book called *Amazing Grace*? What does "amazing" mean and how does Grace fit this description?

Synthesis Level
- Write a story, poem, or song about being persistent. Dedicate it to Grace.
- Write a letter to Grace; tell Grace why you admire her.

Evaluation Level
- In your opinion, is it okay for Grace to play Peter Pan? Explain your response.

	Knowledge	Comprehension	Application
Contributions	Name two stereotypes that someone might have about Blacks. Write a sentence using the word "discrimination" or "stereotype."	What other words also mean "to discriminate"? What are other words for "stereotype"?	Use the thesaurus to find other words for "stereotype" and "discrimination."
Additive	Define discrimination. Define stereotype.	Share one example of discrimination from the book. What do our laws say about discrimination based on race?	Find our school district's statement or policy about non-discrimination.
Transformation	Identify at least one feeling that Grace had when classmates told her that she could not play Peter Pan.	Describe how it feels to be treated unfairly.	Find another book about discrimination to share with classmates. Find something (e.g., look on face, comment) in the story that suggests how Grace felt about the students' comments.
Social Action	What suggestions do you have for the teacher for handling the students' comments?	What would you do if someone treated you unfairly?	Write a letter to Grace's teacher or principal about the need to have a discrimination policy and statement.

Figure 3.3. **Applying the Ford-**

Analysis	Synthesis	Evaluation
How might Grace's decisions help to improve the lives of other Black children?	Create a song or poem about the book. Capture the main idea of the book using a proverb.	What is your favorite part of the book? Why? What do you like or dislike about Grace? About her family?
How do stereotypes develop? How was Grace discriminated against? The Golden Rule says treat others as you would like to be treated. How did Grace's classmates break this rule? What does this statement mean: "We do not discriminate based on race or national origin." Why do we have laws against discrimination?	Write a short story or poem about treating others fairly.	Why do you think the author wrote this book? Do you think the author has ever faced discrimination or been stereotyped? Explain. Which do you believe is more harmful, stereotypes about race or gender? How do you think Grace might respond to this question? How might her response be similar to or different from your response? Are equal rights and anti-discrimination laws necessary? Explain.
How do you think Grace felt when the students commented that she could not play Peter Pan because she was Black? Read "What happens to a Dream Deferred" by Langston Hughes. What is the message of the poem? How does this poem relate to Grace?	Using your imagination, write a short speech that reflects what Dr. Martin Luther King would have said to Grace about persistence and dreaming. Create a new version of the book in which students do not have stereotypes about Grace.	Do you agree that a Black person (or Grace) should not be allowed to play Peter Pan? Why? How do you feel about laws against discrimination? Do you think minority groups feel the same way? Explain.
What can you (we) do to decrease stereotypes and discrimination in our school or classroom?	Create a classroom policy or rule about treating classmates with fairness and respect.	Conduct a study with classmates about ways to improve race relations in your school building. Share the results with the principal.

Harris Matrix to *Amazing Grace*

- What did you like or dislike about the book? Why?
- Do you think Grace is a role model? Explain.
- Would you recommend this book to other students? Why?
- Evaluate the statement: "Don't judge a book by its cover."

Guiding Questions/Experiences Using the Ford-Harris Matrix

The questions and activities Figure 3.3 are based on the Ford-Harris Matrix. We do not expect teachers to address every item (question, statement, and activity) in the matrix. The examples in each cell serve as a guide for teachers; additional questions, statements, and activities can be added to meet the goals and objectives of each classroom. That is, teachers should select those questions, statements, and activities that meet their particular goals and objectives. However, every effort should be made to address higher levels of the matrix when working with gifted students.

Summary and Conclusions

The need for educators to create educational experiences that challenge gifted students in general and gifted minority students in particular is clear. Too often, teachers who wish to teach gifted students have not been formally prepared to do so; similarly, those who work with students of color may know little about multicultural education. In both instances, teachers run the risk of miseducating students. For instance, we recently read a lesson by a teacher who stated that "American Indians were the only group who did not immigrate to the United States. All other people in America are immigrants." Of course, this is inaccurate because slaves (that is, Blacks) were not immigrants.

The framework/matrix presented in this chapter and described in more depth elsewhere (Ford & Harris, 1999) provides educators with a resource—a model—for developing strategies and learning experiences that meet two important educational goals: (a) challenging students cognitively and academically and (b) preparing students for an increasingly diverse society. Similarly, by focusing on multicultural content, concepts, and issues, the framework gives minority students opportunities to see themselves reflected in the curriculum. It also gives other students ongoing opportunities to see culturally diverse students reflected in the curriculum. Diversity abounds in school settings. Educators must be prepared to work proactively with their students.

References

Banks, J. A. (1994). *An introduction to multicultural education.* Boston: Allyn and Bacon.

Bloom, B. (Ed.). (1956). *Taxonomy of educational objectives. Handbook I: Cognitive domain.* New York: Wiley.

Ford, D. Y., & Harris III, J. J. (1999). *Multicultural gifted education.* New York: Teachers College Press.

Grant, C., & Sleeter, C. (1998). *Turning on learning: Five approaches for multicultural teaching plans for race, class, gender, and disability* (2nd ed.). Columbus, OH: Merrill.

Hoffman, M. (1991). *Amazing grace.* New York: Dial.

Ladson-Billings, G. (1990). Culturally relevant teaching. *College Board Review, 155,* 20–25.

Shade, B. J., Kelly, C., & Oberg, M. (1997). *Creating culturally responsive classrooms.* Washington, DC: American Psychological Association.

Valdez, A. (1999). *Learning in living color: Using literature to incorporate multicultural education into the primary curriculum.* Boston: Allyn and Bacon.

chapter 4

The Challenge of "Challenged Books"

by **Robert Seney**

he joy of reading offers students the opportunity to explore the world through books, and many, if not most, gifted students are avid readers (Halsted, 1993). In fact, reading often becomes their coping skill of choice. They read to handle the lack of challenge and boredom of classrooms that are not meeting their learning needs (the novel behind the textbook is a common scenario). Several studies have reported that gifted students read three or four times as many books as average children (Whitehead, 1984). In addition, gifted students read a greater variety of books and are more adventurous in exploring different types of literature. They read to satisfy their own curiosity and to build their own knowledge bases at a depth that is way beyond what is covered in the classroom. They also read just for the joy of reading.

So, what happens when quality literature is made unavailable by special interest groups or school boards? The result is another limit being placed on gifted students. These students read with more sophistication and understanding than their same-age peers. They often need a book for their own research or to meet their own social and emotional needs. What happens if that book has been taken off the shelf?

The issue of challenged books and censorship is addressed with some trepidation, but for the sake of gifted readers, this anti-intellectual practice that limits gifted students must be addressed. First, the caveats: This chapter addresses the issue of *gifted* students and their available reading selections. Second, the concept of "developmentally appropriate reading" and how that should guide teachers and parents in making appropriate choices of reading materials for students is acknowledged and accepted. However, it is important to realize that "developmentally appropriate" must be redefined for gifted readers. Third, parents should have the right to be involved in the selection of literature for their children. Parents should challenge a book only after they understand the learning objectives or purpose for the selection of that piece of literature and only after they have read the novel itself. This issue will be addressed later.

The first task is to understand the nature of censorship. Even though this chapter addresses "challenges," in fact the issue is censorship. Freud defined *censorship* as "the psychological force that represses ideas, impulses, and feelings and prevents them from entering consciousness in their original form" (as cited in Naylor, 1986, p. 616). In that sense, everyone is a censor. However, the censors who make the headlines are those who are more concerned with political action. They want to suppress ideas that are personally repellent to them and to promulgate their own ideology to the exclusion of other ideologies. The reason usually cited for this suppression and exclusion is "the protection of children"; however, this type of statement is intended to appeal to the emotions. Who doesn't want to protect children? But, of course, protection is not really the issue; rather, suppression and exclusion are. My position is, that, in order for parents and teachers to nurture their gifted children "in the market place of ideas," all ideas must be available—including those concerning abuse, sexuality, and violence.

Broderick (1986) suggested,

Censorship of books and other learning resource materials sends a mixed message to students. On the one hand, we say, read; on the other, we say but don't read this, that, or the other title. A major reason we want children to become dedicated readers is so they will develop judgment, the ability to discern the good from the bad, the superior from the shoddy. (p. 614)

It is well known how quickly gifted students pick up on mixed messages. Silverman (1993) beautifully illustrated this characteristic in her discussion of *perceptiveness*. She defined this concept as "the insight, the intuition, and the ability to read several layers of feeling simultaneously and the ability to quickly get to the core of an issue" (p. 41). Therefore, it is easy to see how it is possible for gifted students to lose their confidence when they receive the mixed messages that are inherent in censorship issues.

The National Council of Teachers of English (NCTE), in its position statement "Students' Right to Read" (http://www. ncte.org/about/over/positions/category/cens/107616.htm), makes two observations about censorship. First, any work is potentially open to attack by someone, somewhere, sometime, for some reason. For example, since one parent in a New Jersey school district complained that a dictionary used sexually explicit terms in its definitions, it was removed. The second observation is that censorship is often arbitrary and irrational. One example here is that a classic pre-Christian Greek text was challenged because it was "un-Christian."

In 1978, the NCTE identified several forms of censorship in a brochure (see Figure 4.1). Because censorship takes many forms, teachers and parents must be diligent in making sure that appropriate literature and information are available for gifted learners. When specific works are not available, demand to see the rationalization for the censorship.

Obviously, conflict, especially between teachers and parents, should be avoided; therefore, it is important to have in place a process that will deal with potential problems. Figure 4.2 offers a classroom guide that may help to avoid possible challenges surrounding literature selected for study. This guide was developed by the author using his classroom experience and guidelines from the NCTE (see http://www.ncte.org).

One recommended strategy is for parents and children to read the questioned book together and then discuss it. This gives

1. **Subtle censorship by "selection" of novels.** In this form, only those novels that meet the censor's specific criteria are selected for the classroom or reading list.

2. **Deliberate exclusion of certain books.** Because the censor (teacher, parent, or a public group) is aware of issues or content, identified books are deliberately excluded from the library, classroom, and approved lists.

3. **Alteration of books.** Many students laugh about the books with missing pages and the "blacked" out words and phrases that teachers or librarians have mutilated. But, to be fair, this is usually done because of parental pressure. Students are not fooled, and the irony is that they often hear worse situations and language in the hall, in the street, and on television.

4. **Required book lists.** Certainly, this might be the most sophisticated use of censorship. It is generally believed that the professional in the field certainly knows what is best for students to read, and for the most part this is true. However, other motives may be at work here. The omissions and selections for the lists may have to be questioned from time to time.

5. **Suppression of materials as a result of community pressure.** It is so easy to pull a book off the shelf when a few people object. Again, the question must be asked what are the motives and have all the consequences of this form of censorship been truly considered?

6. **Direct edict.** This form of censorship is probably the easiest for the teacher or the librarian to handle: "They made me do it!" Groups approach school boards, and, hoping to forego any confrontation, the board will rule to remove, cut, or prohibit the targeted book. Again, the consequences of such actions are usually not thought out.

7. **Deliberate omission.** This is a more subtle form of deliberate exclusion. It is easy to claim innocence and ignorance in not providing a specific book or leaving it off a reading list.

8. **Curtailment.** Curtailment is an extension of suppression of materials and may just be a softer version of suppression. In this case, the availability or access to a particular book is limited. It's here, but not everyone gets a chance to look at it.

Figure 4.1. **Forms of censorship**

1. At the beginning of the year, provide parents a list of the novels that will be used in the classroom.

2. Define the philosophy of reading to be followed in the classroom and explain that student choice for additional reading is important (Carlsen & Sherrill, 1988) and that choice of those novels is between students and parents.

3. Have a written rationale for every classroom novel that will be used.

4. Define the learning goals for each novel.

5. Encourage parents to read the novels and discuss them with their students.

6. If there is a problem, ask the parents to suggest an alternative that will meet the designated learning objectives.

Figure 4.2. Censorship: A classroom guide

parents an opportunity to state objections to the book, content, or issue from the point of view of their own values and, at the same time, not deny the child the opportunity to read the questioned novel. In this way, parents can build a strong reading bond with their children, and they have the opportunity to teach their children a sense of the moral values they hold. To keep parents informed, teachers may want to address concerns about particular books in parent meetings and in their classrooms. If this is the case, the known objections and their reasons should be carefully listed. This also provides teachers with an opportunity to discuss the issue of selecting appropriate reading materials for students.

Teachers who take up the task of addressing challenged books and are willing to have students read sensitive books in their classrooms must be willing and prepared to discuss these books with students. This means they may have to deal with some difficult issues; therefore, they must be personally comfortable with openly discussing topics that may be sensitive or embarrassing. Teachers must also create a classroom environment where it is safe to have an open and frank discussion (Hunt & Seney, 2001).

Teachers must be prepared by doing their homework. They should know the community and its values, and they should prepare for possible challenges to a book (Bushman & Parks-Haas, 2001). The written rationale is very important. Bushman and Parks-Haas (p. 252) suggested eight elements that should be included in a rationale:

1. For what class is this book especially appropriate?
2. To what particular objective—literary, psychological, or pedagogical—does this book lend itself?
3. In what ways will the book be used to meet those objectives?
4. What problems of style, tone, or theme in the book are possible grounds for censorship?
5. How does the teacher plan to meet those problems?
6. Assuming that the objectives are met, how would students be different because of reading this book?
7. What are some other appropriate books an individual student might read in place of this book?
8. What reputable sources have recommended this book? What have critics said of it? (This answer should cite reviews, if any are available.)

It is also important to note that the more choices students have in reading or not reading specific titles, the less potential there is for censorship or challenge (Bushman & Parks-Haas). The prepared teacher will have alternate assignments and titles in mind.

Teachers who follow these procedures will have few problems with parents about the choice of literature. It is crucial to create the communication link between classrooms and parents as early in the year as possible. How should the occasional problem be addressed? I have used the following steps:

1. Arrange for a parent conference.
2. Be sure to ask if the parent has read the entire book.
3. Make sure that the parent understands the goals and objectives for using this particular book.
4. Ask the parent to list his or her objections to the novel as completely as possible.
5. Provide a written rationale and defense of the use of the novel.

6. If there is still a problem, ask the parent to suggest an alternative and appropriate novel that will meet the designated learning objectives.
7. Respect parents' values.
8. Make sure the student does not get caught in the middle of a disagreement.

Again, NCTE guidelines have been helpful in creating this process.

In the few cases in which I have had parents object to a particular book, the parent had not read it in its entirety. It is important to make it clear that both teachers and parents are wasting time in discussing the situation if the book has not been read. This is a good time to give to the parents the "Citizen's Request for Reconsideration of a Work" form designed by the NCTE and available at the end of its position statement "The Student's Right to Read" (http://www.ncte.org/about/over/positions/level/gen/107616.htm). Ask the parents to complete the form after they have read the book and before the next conference. It has been my experience that, in nearly every case in which this process was followed, parents withdrew their objections. In one situation, the parent even became a champion for a book that is often challenged.

Gifted middle school and high school students are often interested in the issue of censorship. This may be because they have been frustrated so often in their own pursuit of knowledge. They seem to identify readily with the lack of "fairness" that censorship often creates, which presents a good opportunity for both teachers and parents who are guiding gifted students in independent study. This interest also creates the opportunity for teachers and students to design a great unit of study on this issue, which can be based on young adult literature. The following is a list of novels that deal with the issue of censorship in various ways:

- *Nothing But the Truth* (Avi, 1991)
- *Fahrenheit 451* (Ray Bradbury, 1966)
- *The Year They Burned the Books* (Nancy Garden, 1999)
- *The Day They Came to Arrest the Book* (Nat Hentoff, 1982)
- *The Ninth Issue* (Dallin Malmgren, 1989)

- *The Last Safe Place on Earth* (Richard Peck, 1995)
- *The Last Book in the Universe* (Rodman Philbrick, 2000)
- *Save Halloween* (Stephanie Tolen, 1993)

Reading these novels and discussing them can easily be the basis of an interdisciplinary, differentiated curriculum unit.

It might be argued that challenged books and censorship are two different issues. In fact, the American Library Association has drawn a difference between *challenging* and *banning* books, both forms of *censorship*. "A challenge is an attempt to remove or restrict materials based upon the objections of a person or group. A banning is the removal of those materials. Challenges do not simply involve a person expressing a point-of-view; rather they are an attempt to remove material from the curriculum or library, thereby *restricting the access* [emphasis added] of others" (http://www.ala.org/ala/oif/bannedbooksweek/challengedbanned/challengedbanned.htm).

Educators must be careful not to place any more restrictions upon gifted students. Since many successful gifted students direct the majority of their own learning, teachers and parents must not limit their access to information, whether for research or for the joy of reading. They live with too many limits as it is. It is the duty of teachers and parents of gifted students to challenge any person or group that seeks to challenge or ban any book and thereby restrict the access of knowledge, enjoyment, and intellectual development.

Reference List

Baskin, B., & Harris, K. (1980). *Books for the gifted child.* New York: Bowker.

Broderick, D. (1986). *Areas and issues: Children and books.* In Z. Sutherland & M. Arbuthnot (Eds.), *Children and books* (7th ed., pp. 614–615). Glenview, IL: Foresman.

Bushman, J., & Parks-Haas, K. (2001). *Using young adult literature in the English classroom* (3rd ed). Columbus, OH: Prentice Hall.

Carlsen, R., & Sherrill, A. (1988). *Voices of readers: How we come to love books.* Urbana, IL: National Council of Teachers of English.

Halsted, J. (1993). *Some of my best friends are books: Guiding gifted readers from pre-school to high school.* Dayton: Ohio Psychology Press.

Hunt, B., & Seney, R. (2001). Planning the learning environment. In
F. A. Karnes & S. M. Bean (Eds.), *Methods and materials for teaching the gifted* (pp. 43–89). Waco TX: Prufrock Press.

Naylor, A (1986). Censorship. In Z. Sutherland & M. Arbuthnot
(Eds.), *Children and books* (7th ed., pp. 615–622). Glenview, IL:
Foresman.

National Council for Teachers of English (NCTE). (1978).
Censorship: Don't let it become an issue in your schools. [Brochure].
Urbana, IL: Author.

Silverman, L. K. (1993). *Counseling the gifted and talented.* Denver,
CO: Love.

Whitehead, R. (1984). *A guide to selecting books for children.* Metuchen,
NJ: Scarecrow.

Appendix: All-Time Top 10 Favorites

I am a very active reader in the genre of young adult literature. I
see this quality literature as a means to provide a perfect match to
the verbal characteristics of gifted students, to Halsted's (1994)
characteristics of books most appropriate for gifted readers, and to
the characteristics of contemporary young adult literature. I share
my new reading list each year at various conferences. The following
is my list of all-time favorite young adult novels.

- *What Child is This* by Caroline Cooney (Delacorte Press;
  ISBN 0–440-50057-5)
- *Fade* by Robert Cormier (Delacorte Press; ISBN 0-440-
  50057-5)
- *Salamandastron** by Brian Jacques (Philomel Books; ISBN
  0-399-21992-7)
- *Gathering Blue* by Lois Lowry (Houghton Mifflin: ISBN 0-
  6187-05581-9)
- *Bridge to Terabithia* by Katherine Paterson (Avon Books;
  ISBN 0-380-43281-1)
- *Dogsong* by Gary Paulsen (Bradbury Press; ISBN 0-02-
  770180-8)
- *The Van Gogh Café* by Cynthia Rylant (Harcourt Brace;
  ISBN 0-15-200843-8)
- *Interstellar Pig* by William Sleator (Peter Smith Pub; ISBN
  0-844-66898-2)

- *Welcome to the Ark* by Stephanie Tolan (Morrow Junior Books; ISBN 0-688-13724-5)
- *A Solitary Blue* by Cynthia Voight (Ballentine Books; ISBN 0-449-70115-8)

Note. *Whole series a special favorite.

Integrating Drama With Literature

chapter 5

Using Creative Dramatics With Gifted Students

by **Andrew P. Johnson**

reative dramatics are effective learning tools to use with highly creative and intellectually gifted students. They are an active learning experience that are fun and open-ended and use high-level thinking to synthesize storylines and create dialogue. This chapter provides specific instructions for using creative dramatics in the classroom.

What Are Creative Dramatics?

Creative dramatics build on a student's imagination and willingness to act or pretend in order to reinforce academic, emotional, and interpersonal objectives (Froese, 1996). They are a form of imaginative play that helps students learn. Creative dramatics use no written dialogue, which makes it different from doing a play (Block, 1997; Edwards, 1997; Heining, 1993; Kelner, 1993). In a play, actors read or memorize lines that someone else wrote. In creative dramatics, actors create and use their own words to convey meaning. Although teachers provide a beginning structure, students who use creative dramatics are encouraged to improvise or change the original form (Edwards, 1997; Heining, 1993; Kelner, 1993).

Why Use Creative Dramatics?

Creative dramatics engage students from all levels and abilities. Thus, they are a perfect tool to use in differentiating the curriculum for highly creative and intellectually gifted students. It promotes the intellectual development of young children by linking the world of play and imagination to the world of reason and knowledge (Froese, 1996; Kelner, 1993).

For students of all ages, creative dramatics promote language and vocabulary growth (Block, 1997; Edwards, 1997; Froese, 1996; Heining, 1993; Kelner, 1993), stimulate imagination and creative thinking (Block; Kelner), and foster critical thinking and higher level cognitive processes (Cox, 1983; Harp, 1988; Kelner; Miller & Mason, 1983; Wagner, 1988; Yaffee, 1989). Here, students must think out loud, organize and synthesize information, interpret ideas, create new ideas, and interact cooperatively with others.

Creative dramatics also give students a sense of ownership of their learning (Froese, 1996). The teacher steps offstage and allows students to have the central focus. The improvisational nature of creative dramatics ensures that children are the decision makers and take an active role in planning and shaping the learning event (Block, 1997). In this sense, creative dramatics serve to empower students (Miller & Mason, 1983; Verriour, 1990; Wolf, 1993; Yaffee, 1989).

Components of Creative Dramatics

There are four necessary components to creative dramatics: (a) structure, (b) open-endedness, (c) a safe environment, and (d) feedback.

Structure

While pretending is natural for children, improvising a short drama can be a difficult and abstract process. Children need structure to guide their actions and dialogue during the initial stages of creative dramatics. Teachers can provide this structure by modeling and demonstrating the basic story, actions, possible dialogue, and characterizations. It is best to keep early dramas short and simple by using only two to four characters. Older students and those with experience in creative dramatics will need less structure.

Open-Endedness

Creative dramatics are spontaneous and changeable. Although it works best when teachers provide a beginning structure, this structure should be flexible and open-ended. As students become more comfortable with creative dramatics, they will begin to use ideas and experiences from their own lives to create unique variations on the original themes. Using a prepared script would not allow this to happen. It is a good rule, therefore, never to use written dialogue. Provide structure, but let students find their own words to carry the meaning and encourage improvisation and alternate endings.

A Safe Environment

Creativity of any kind involves a certain amount of risk and disclosure. Creativity is enhanced when the teacher creates a fun, safe environment. Closing the classroom door during the initial learning stages of creative dramatics can help to develop a sense of safety and community. A teacher who is willing to take creative risks by modeling and participating in creative dramatics primes the pump for further creative endeavors. Also, feedback that is positive and specific and acknowledges actors and their efforts will ensure that creative behaviors continue. Finally, a teacher should never force students to participate in creative dramatics; rather, he or she should always ask for volunteers.

Feedback

Students like to receive both formal and informal feedback. Informal feedback is best given by a teacher's response in reacting to the drama, laughing when appropriate, and giving other verbal and nonverbal responses. More formal feedback is given when a drama has ended. Here, the teacher processes the experience with students and recognizes actors for those things done well. As students become more familiar with the feedback process, they become better able to reflect upon these experiences and describe successful and less successful dramatic elements. Actors of all ages eventually develop a critical eye and become adept at giving each other positive feedback. Feedback is most effective when it focuses on the four actor's elements.

Actor's Elements

The actor's elements are the specific tools actors use to create characters. Students enjoy learning about the craft of acting and seeing how each of these elements can be used effectively. The four actor's elements utilized in creative dramatics are (a) voice, (b) body, (c) character or imagination, and (d) group work.

Voice

The voice is an important tool for an actor. In using the voice, actors must attend to volume, rate, pitch, and tone.

First, can you hear the actor? Does he or she speak in a loud voice? The teacher can help students by describing the difference between a speaking voice and an acting voice. While engaging actors in a dialogue at the front of the room, it is sometimes helpful for the teacher to move to the back of the room. This reinforces the idea that students must project to the whole room. Second, does the actor speak slowly enough to be understood? When students are nervous, it is easy to speak too fast. Third, do they vary their pitch? High and low vocal exercises that focus on pitch, such as fire engine sounds or sentences with high and low parts, are effective ways to develop a feeling for pitch. Finally, students need to be taught how to develop character voices that vary in tone. Here, the learner can explore the sounds different animals or characters might make (see Figure 5.1). Vocal exercises such as these make good warm-ups or sponge activities while helping students focus on this element.

Individual or small groups of students will repeat one or more of the lines below. Ask them to project or portray a particular quality or character as they speak each sentence.

Qualities or Characters

Scared, humorous, mysterious, large, surprised, small, painful, happy, angry, nervous, evil, kind, heavy, light, a lion, a hippo, a giraffe, a crocodile, a wolf, a mouse, an elephant, a cow, an ice cube, the Wicked Witch of the West, the Good Witch Glinda, the tooth fairy, a king/queen, a robot, a teacher, a smart kid, a spoiled kid, a strong kid, a high voice, a low voice, a shaky voice, a flat voice, a nasal voice, a wide voice, a fast voice, a slow voice, a loud voice, a quiet voice.

Example

Say in a very mysterious way, "Are you going to wear the red cap to the fair?"
Say in a very angry way, "Are you going to wear the red cap to the fair?"
Use a flat voice to say, "Are you going to wear the red cap to the fair?"
Use a mouse voice to say, "Are you going to wear the red cap to the fair?"

Sentences

1. Are you going to wear the red cap to the fair?
2. There's a mouse in the bathtub and she's brushing her teeth.
3. I've lost my book and I don't know where to find it.
4. You're stepping on my foot.
5. There's a fly in my vanilla pudding!
6. I want to go home.

Figure 5.1. **Vocal exercises**

Body

Actors need to learn how to use their whole body, as well as their face, to create a character or express a feeling. Teachers can help students focus specifically on the body in five ways.

First, they can have students do a silent spot where they pantomime various activities (see Figure 5.2). Second, a bulletin board called "Face Place" can be put up showing many different faces and expressions. Third, students can practice using their face and body to react silently to others as they speak their lines

1. Walk like an elephant, feather, grasshopper, cooked spaghetti, uncooked spaghetti, a quiet mouse, or like a careful chicken.
2. Blow a bubble, catch it in the air, and then set it down very carefully on the table.
3. Walk in the kitchen, take a jar of pickles out of the refrigerator, open the jar and eat one. It is very sour.
4. Brush your teeth in the morning.
5. Prepare and eat ice cream with spinach on top.
6. Come into a room, look around, and hide in the closet.
7. You are walking through a room, and your foot gets stuck on some glue. You sit down to think and other parts of you get stuck.
8. You're a mouse looking at some cheese on a mousetrap. Take it off very carefully.
9. Lift something heavy, light, smelly, gooey, small, big, wiggly, or shaky.
10. Tell a story without using any voice.
11. Using only your face, show anger, surprise, fatigue, hurt, fear, humor, sluggishness, or someone who just heard a loud noise.

Figure 5.2. **Physical drama exercises**

or perform an action. Fourth, different ways of walking or moving can be explored. Finally, students can dramatize or act out various situations without using their voice.

Character or Imagination

This element is concerned with the student's ability to make a character believable. Does the actor stay in character? Does she or he react when others are talking? Is the actor able to become somebody other than him- or herself? Does the actor walk, talk, and move like that character? Is the actor believable without being too silly? Teach students to stay in character and be believable at all times. Figure 5.3 shows some activities that are designed to get students to think about specific character traits.

Group Work

Once students are comfortable with creative dramatics, they will be able to work independently in small groups. In one class period, a teacher will eventually be able to introduce a drama,

The actor(s) will create a short scene in an interesting and imaginative way. These can be done with or without sound.

Scenarios

1. You are a wicked wolf with a pig that is not very smart. Play both characters and show your audience a different way the wolf might have gotten into the pig's house.
2. You are Chicken Little walking around the chicken yard eating seeds. A pinecone hits you on the head. Show the audience how you will react and what you will do next.
3. You are on the playground playing when the Wicked Witch of the West appears. She thinks your shoes are magic and she wants them. Show the audience what happens.
4. The Loudmouth family is eating breakfast. Show the audience what this looks and sounds like.
5. You are a mouse who is very hungry. While looking for cheese, your foot gets stuck in some glue. Show how you will react and how you will solve the problem.
6. You are a prince or princess who hates getting dirty. You accidentally get some mud on your clothes. Show how you might react and what you will do to solve the problem.
7. You are a troll who is very sweet and lovable. Show what might happen if you meet a billy goat on a bridge.
8. You are a timid zebra. A crabby lion is standing on your foot. What will you do?

Figure 5.3. **Exercises to develop character or imagination**

model and explain it, send groups of three or four students off into different parts of the room to practice, and then bring everybody back to perform and process their dramas.

Social or interpersonal skills can be taught here in order to make this a more successful endeavor. Does everyone feel a part of the group? Does everyone have a chance to share ideas? Do the actors take turns? Are they all on-task and contributing? Is the group working together? Do the actors react to each other? Making students aware of this actor's element will help to avoid much of the pandemonium that may occur when students are working in small groups. Group work also provides an additional opportunity to teach and review social skills.

Final Thoughts

Creative dramatics can help meet the needs of highly creative and intellectually gifted students. Here are four final ideas to consider when beginning:

1. First, allow students to become comfortable with this process slowly. Use creative dramatics no more than two or three times a week.
2. Second, consider using creative dramatics right before lunch or toward the end of the day when students are apt to be restless and need a chance to move.
3. Third, students love to perform for their peers. Therefore, it is easy to send small groups of actors to other classrooms to do quick 5-minute dramas.
4. Finally, remember that creative dramatics should be enjoyable learning experiences.

References

Block, C. C. (1997). *Teaching the language arts: Expanding thinking through student-centered instruction.* Needham Heights, MA: Allyn and Bacon.

Cox, C. (1983). Forum: Informal classroom drama. *Language Arts, 60,* 370–372.

Edwards, L. C. (1997). *The creative arts: A process approach for teachers and children.* Upper Saddle River, NJ: Simon & Schuster.

Froese, V. (1996). *Whole-language: Practice and theory* (2nd ed.). Needham Heights, MA: Allyn and Bacon.

Harp, B. (1988). When the principal asks: "Is all that drama taking valuable time away from reading?" *The Reading Teacher, 41,* 938–940.

Heining, R. B. (1993). *Creative drama for the classroom teacher* (4th ed.). Englewood Cliffs, NJ: Simon & Schuster.

Kelner, L. B. (1993). *The creative classroom: A guide for using creative drama in the classroom PreK–6.* Portsmouth, NH: Heinemann.

Miller, G. M., & Mason, G. E. (1983). Dramatic improvisation: Risk-free role playing for improving reading performance. *The Reading Teacher, 37,* 128–131.

Verriour, P. (1990). Storying and storytelling in drama. *Language Arts, 67,* 144–149.

Wagner, B. J. (1988). Research currents: Does classroom drama affect the arts of language? *Language Arts, 65,* 46–55.

Wolf, S. A. (1993). What's in a name? Labels and literacy in readers theatre. *The Reading Teacher, 46,* 540–545.

Yaffee, S. H. (1989). Drama as a teaching tool. *Educational Leadership, 46,* 29–32.

chapter 6

Dramatic Prelude

*using drama to introduce
classic literature to young readers*

by **Anita Winstead**

hen I first announced to my third-grade students
that we would be reading literary works by Charles
Dickens and William Shakespeare, there were quite
a few puzzled looks on their faces. Here's how we
eliminated the frustration and intimidation that
sometimes arises when you mention these authors.

My class produced two exciting dramatic projects
as an introduction to classic literature. By writing and
presenting their own adaptation of Charles Dickens'
A Christmas Carol and William Shakespeare's *The
Tempest*, they learned about the playwriting process,
enhanced their ability to work as a team, and developed a better appreciation for these two outstanding
authors.

The Making of *A Holiday Carol*

We began our first project by reading a con-
densed version of *A Christmas Carol* and then compared and contrasted it to various movie and
television adaptations. Next, we read the biography

Charles Dickens: The Man Who Had Great Expectations (Stanley & Vennema, 1993). The class talked about Dickens' difficult childhood and compared some of the societal issues of his time (i.e., child labor) to our present society (i.e., homelessness).

The students learned that the message from *A Christmas Carol* was to honor the spirit of Christmas year-round, so we asked parents to send in gently used clothing and toys that we delivered to a local homeless shelter. Later in the year, we made Valentine cards for a children's hospital and again donated more clothing items to a homeless shelter.

To experience writing a professional dramatic play, I contracted a local playwright. Together, we divided the story into three acts and discussed what happened at the beginning, middle, and end. The class participated in conversations about each character and the most important elements of the story. We decided that our version of *A Christmas Carol* would be set in the present and would have a multicultural theme and characters.

The students wanted the Scrooge character to discover the joy of the three major holidays: Christmas, Hanukkah, and Kwanzaa. In the ending, the Cratchit family, friends, and Scrooge all join together at the Cratchit home on the make-believe eve of the three holidays to celebrate the traditions of Christmas, Hanukkah, and Kwanzaa together.

After the students had listed each character and discussed what took place in each act of Dickens' version of the story, it was their turn to write their own version. They were divided into three groups with the task of writing the scenes and dialogue for the characters in each act. Each group shared ideas and then decided what should take place in each scene and what each character should say. They needed about three 45-minute sessions to complete this task. I monitored and offered advice when they needed it, but they did most of it on their own.

Once the scenes and dialogue were written for each act, all three acts were put together in a first draft, and a typed copy of our script was provided for each student. As a class, we read and reread the script, made revisions, and corrected grammar and spelling together. Then, we settled on a new title for our play: *A Holiday Carol*.

Most of the students chose the part they wanted to play. For example, the part of Tiny Tim was chosen by a female student, so we renamed that character Tiny Tina. The class added more characters and dialogue so that each student could have a speaking role. We voted to audition for Scrooge's part, however, since it was such a popular role.

Once we had finalized our script, the students practiced memorizing their lines in class and at home. The class gave suggestions for scenery and musical selections, and they had their parents help provide costumes and props. A local drama coach was contracted to assist the students with stage presence, voice projection, stage blocking, finding a point of focus, theatrical make-up, and other dramatization skills. The coach also suggested the special effect of using a fog machine during the cemetery scene and when the ghosts made their entrances. The students and the audience were quite excited about that!

There was an authentic audience as the class performed their adaptation for our school's student body and parents. After the performance, all of the cast members sat on stage and answered questions from the audience, such as "How long did it take to prepare your play?" and "How did Scrooge memorize all of those lines?" The class was also thrilled to do a performance at a small, local dinner theater for another school's drama club. Soon afterwards the class attended a local professional theater to see a live performance of a *A Christmas Carol*. After that performance, I had arranged for some of the professional actors to participate in a question-and-answer session with our class and for the stage manager to give us a backstage tour.

Introducing Shakespeare

In the spring, we followed a similar process for our dramatization of William Shakespeare's play, *The Tempest*, which is about a magical duke who is exiled and then stranded on an enchanted island for 12 years with his beautiful daughter, a spirit, and a monster. When the duke's enemies are washed ashore on the island after a violent tempest, he uses his magical powers to confront them.

After reading author Bruce Colville's beautifully written and illustrated picture-book adaptation *William Shakespeare's The*

Tempest (1994) and Shakespeare's biography, *Bard of Avon: The Story of William Shakespeare* (Stanley & Vennema, 1992), the students commented that they felt two of the reasons Shakespeare was considered a great writer were his ability to make his plays exciting and his use of humor.

Next, we had a local Shakespearean performer visit our class and perform for us. We also took a field trip to a local high school to see their Renaissance Fair. Our class borrowed some of the ideas we gained from these experiences when planning our costumes, theatrical make-up, scenery, music, and special effects. There was less assistance from our playwright and drama coach with this second project so that the class could demonstrate what they had learned about the playwriting process and dramatization earlier in the year.

The students again began working in small groups. We decided to write a monologue for each Shakespearean character. They had learned that young boys would perform the female roles in plays performed during the Elizabethan period, so it was a sign of the times to have a female student choose to play the role of Shakespeare, our narrator.

Students auditioned for the 13 challenging, but popular roles. For this performance, each individual character was alone on center stage. They introduced themselves and told what part they played in this adventure from their own point of view. Performing a series of monologues proved to be much more challenging than a play using dialogue. It required more intense practice for the students to memorize lines and be convincing as their characters. I encouraged them throughout rehearsals. They worked hard, but they enjoyed it and you could see their growth in this second production.

Since this play mentioned a ship that was washed ashore on an enchanted island by a violent storm, the students rewrote the lyrics to the *Gilligan's Island* theme song as a charming introduction to this presentation (the lyrics to the song, as well as the entire text of the production, are included at the end of the chapter). Four students sang the introductory song while the others acted as the elements of wind, waves, rain, thunder, and lightning. The students added the sound effects of wind and thunder by inviting members of our school's musical percussion group to perform. I rented a powerful strobe light from a theatrical supplier to produce the visual effect of lightning. The crashing cymbals, drums, and intense lighting made the production even more fun to watch.

Before we performed this production for the school, we asked our librarian to read Bruce Colville's (1994) picture-book adaptation of *The Tempest* to every class so that the entire student body would better understand and enjoy our performance.

Conclusion

Using drama to enhance the study of Charles Dickens and William Shakespeare was a worthy project because both productions went beyond fulfilling the immediate goals of learning the playwriting process, teamwork, and literature appreciation. For example, the students were inspired by Dickens to help the homeless, which, in turn, made them feel good about themselves.

All students were enthusiastically involved, worked together, and encouraged each others' ideas during the creation of both of these projects. The students displayed growth in self-esteem as they improved their dramatization skills and overcame the challenge of standing in front of a large audience and successfully delivering their lines.

Teamwork also included parental involvement. Parents helped their children with memorizing their lines, and many provided costumes. One parent volunteered to make copies of the video we made of each production, which we sold as a fundraiser.

The overriding benefits of these two unforgettable projects are that the students now have a better appreciation for Dickens and Shakespeare. I noticed them asking the librarian about other books written by these authors after we had completed our productions. We also heightened the students' awareness by performing our dramatic presentations schoolwide and within the community. I think they have truly demonstrated that the classics can be enjoyable.

References

Colville, B. (1994). *William Shakespeare's The tempest.* New York: Doubleday.

Stanley, D., & Vennema, P. (1992). *Bard of avon: The story of William Shakespeare.* New York: HarperCollins.

Stanley, D., & Vennema, P. (1993). *Charles Dickens: The man who had great expectations.* New York: HarperCollins.

Author Note

Parts of our projects were funded by Creative Connections, a local grant that encourages integration of the arts in school curriculum. Thanks to Jane Dudney of Creative Connections, Barbara Franklin, playwright, and Karen Hunter, drama coach, who helped to make the classics come alive in our classroom.

"Shakespeare's Isle"
(Sung to the tune of "Gilligan's Island Theme")

Just sit right back and you'll hear a tale
A tale of a fateful trip
About the Duke Prospero
And the tempest that he whipped

Prospero was a mighty magician
His daughter Miranda was a dove
And when she first met Ferdinand
We knew it would be love
We knew it would be love

The weather started getting rough
The giant ship was tossed
If not for the courageous but frightened
    crew
The ship would be lost

The ship set ground of the shore of this
Uncharted desert isle
With Caliban
The Jesters, too
Antonio
And James
King Anthony
Stephano and Ariel
Here on Shakespeare's Isle

So this is the tale
Of our castaways
They're here for 12 long years
They'll have to make the best of things
Now that they are here
Prospero and Miranda
They did their very best
To teach them all a lesson
In this tropic island mess

No silver, no gold, no crystal
Not a single luxury
Like living in the stone age
It's primitive as can be

So join us here today my friends
You're sure to get a smile
From 12 stranded castaways
Here on Shakespeare's Isle

The Tempest
as interpreted by Anita Winstead's third-grade class

The Tempest *begins with characters frozen in an attractive pose and smiles on stage. Elements also sit frozen with smiles on the stage steps. Music from the Elizabethan age is playing in background. Music fades. Elements begin their sound effects and gestures. Elements fade. Then Shakespeare comes to life and walks to center stage. All characters use face, hand, and open body gestures when they speak LOUDLY, CLEARLY, and SLOWLY to the audience.*

WILLIMEENA SHAKESPEARE—Welcome ladies and gentlemen. My name is Williameena Shakespeare, and I'd like to tell you about my play, *The Tempest.* A tempest is a storm brought on by a magician. (*Elements sound effects for 30 seconds.*) This story is about the "green-eyed monster"—jealousy! It is also about hate, brother against brother, exile, and—in the end—forgiveness. I'm sure you will like my story. Let me introduce you to the characters of this wonderful play. (*Walks over to Prospero and puts hand on his shoulder.*) First, here's Prospero, the Duke of Milan.

PROSPERO—(*Prospero comes to life and walks to center stage.*) Hello, my name is Prospero. I am a magician who doesn't much care for the duties of being the Duke of Milan. I let my brother do all the work because I find it so bor-r-ring! I much prefer reading and writing, but I am also friendly and full of laughter. I have a daughter named Miranda. She is a sweet, lovely child. My brother is jealous of me and somehow he and the King of Naples plotted against me and sent me and my dear daughter away in a leaking boat. We landed on an island. And if it weren't for a dear friend who gave us food, clothes, and my magic books, we would have drowned. (*Prospero walks back to where Shakespeare is standing, strikes a pose and freezes.*)

SHAKESPEARE—(*Shakespeare is reading his lines as he walks to center stage and then walks over to Miranda.*) That's what he gets for liking magic more than the duties of his job. Look how it affected his sweet daughter Miranda, who was only 3 years old when she went into exile with her father. They both "had seen better days." (*Touches Miranda on the shoulder.*)

MIRANDA—(*Miranda comes to life and walks to center stage.*) My name is Miranda. My father, Prospero, is the Duke of Milan. For a long time we lived on an island. My father freed a spirit named Ariel from a tree, and she became our servant for 12 years. There was also an ugly beast known as Caliban. At first, he was our friend. But when he tried to hurt me, my father made him leave our home. (*Pause*) One day I saw a ship coming. When I told my father about it, he caused a tempest to occur. (*Elements sound effects for 30 seconds.*) I asked my father to stop it, and he did before any great harm was done. Soon after the big ship came, a young man named Ferdinand walked up and spoke to me. I was happy to see him, since I didn't have anyone my age to talk to. My father saw us together and made Ferdinand work for us. I felt sorry for him, and I offered to help. Ferdinand told me that "seeing you gives me great strength." My father came to us and told us that Ferdinand had passed the test and that he approved of our love. He told us that we would be wed. (*Walks back to where Shakespeare stands. Strikes a pose.*)

SHAKESPEARE—(*Walks over to Antonio.*) Next we have Antonio, Prospero's "own flesh and blood." He finally took over his brother's Dukedom by making a pact with the King of Naples to rid the world of Prospero forever. (*Touches Antonio's shoulder.*)

ANTONIO—(*Walks to center stage with mean look on his face.*) My name is Antonio. I am Prospero's brother. I am a nasty, rude person. It's true that I am jealous of my brother. It's also true that I plotted to have Prospero and my niece put on a leaky boat to sail out to sea. Quite frankly, I didn't want them to return, so I could become the Duke. When I heard that Prospero was alive, and I convinced his worst enemy, the King of Naples, to sail in a ship, find him, and destroy him. A great tempest arose. (*Elements sound effects for 30 seconds.*) I landed on an island and thought everyone was dead. I found Miranda and Prospero there. Prospero threatened to harm me, but I begged for forgiveness. He forgave me and gave me back my ship and its crew. (*Return to Shakespeare. Strike a pose.*)

SHAKESPEARE—(*Walks over to James and touches shoulder.*) Now I must introduce you to James, for it was he who helped Prospero and Miranda when they first were exiled.

JAMES—(*Walks to center stage with nice smile.*) My name is James, and I am a 30-year-old kind and generous man who grew up with Prospero. Prospero bought a house for me and my young family. I was able to do a good deed for Prospero when his evil brother sent him away in a leaky boat. I gave him and his daughter clothes, food, and Prospero's magic book and staff. (*Returns to Shakespeare. Strikes a pose.*)

SHAKESPEARE—(*Walks over to Ariel and touches her shoulder.*) Ah, the spirit, Ariel, who Prospero sets free. She helps him do his magic and becomes involved in everything. A loyal servant she is.

ARIEL—(*Floats to center stage.*) My name is Ariel, and I am a spirit. You already know how Prospero freed me, but you may not know why I was there in the first place. The spell was put on me by Caliban's evil mother, Sycorax. I am sweet, kind, and loyal, but also sensitive. I guess anyone would be sensitive if they had been trapped in a tree for 12 years. I was very grateful to Prospero for freeing me, and I offered him anything. Prospero only asked me to be his servant. I agreed, and he promised not to make me do evil things. He also promised to accept me forever as a member of his family. I did easy tasks for Prospero. I spied on his enemies, split them up, and brought Ferdinand and Miranda together. I was loyal to Prospero throughout our time together. I felt sad to see Prospero, Miranda, and the others leave. I wished I could go with them. (*Floats back to Shakespeare. Strikes pose.*)

SHAKESPEARE—(*Walks over to Caliban.*) Let's see. It's time we met Caliban. Caliban is the monster that Prospero befriended when he first came to the island. (*Touches his shoulder then stands back in fear.*)

CALIBAN—(*Hobbles to center stage as he makes monstrous noises.*) My name is Caliban. I am the son of a witch named Sycorax, and I am a disgusting, filthy beast. I have no manners. I was very jealous that Prospero gave his daughter more attention than he gave me! And boy was I mad when he finally kicked me out of his home! No one can change my evil heart. After the famous shipwreck, I met up with a rude butler and some jesters. I led them to Prospero's cave with anger in my heart and tried to kill Prospero. It didn't work. Eventually everyone left the island, and I was left there to dwell alone forever. (*Hobbles back to Shakespeare. Strikes a pose.*)

SHAKESPEARE—(*Walks over to King Anthony and touches shoulder.*) Next, we meet King Anthony of Naples. He was only too pleased to listen to Antonio.

KING ANTHONY OF NAPLES—(*Walks like a snobby king with his nose in the air to center stage.*) I am a king who doesn't keep his word. Prospero is my worst enemy and with the help of Antonio, I ruled Milan! I thought I had sent Prospero to his doom. I was angry when I heard he was alive. Like Antonio, when the ship was caught in the great tempest (*Elements sound effects for 30 seconds*), I was washed ashore. I thought everyone else was dead, including my son. I was very sad. As I walked around the island, I wept for my son's death. When I found Prospero, I also saw that my son was alive, too. I was happy because Prospero forgave me. (*Walks with kingly manner back to Shakespeare. Strikes a pose.*)

SHAKESPEARE—(*Walks to center stage.*) What's a story without a little love? Ferdinand, the king's son, is destined to fall in love with the beautiful Miranda. Who could ever imagine that he would become Prospero's son-in-law? (*Walks over to Ferdinand and touches shoulder.*)

FERDINAND—(*Walks to center stage.*) My name is Ferdinand. My father is the King of Naples. I went with him on that fateful trip to find Prospero. By now I guess you all know that I, too, was washed ashore after the tempest. (*Elements sound effects for 30 seconds.*) I thought everyone else had died, including my father. After walking for a while, I came upon the beautiful Miranda and her father, Prospero. I liked Miranda, but Prospero made me work to prove that I loved her. So I worked until Prospero understood my love for his daughter. When I found out that my father was alive, I was so happy. I married Miranda, and we went back to Milan and lived happily ever after. (*Walks back to Shakespeare. Strikes a pose.*)

SHAKESPEARE—(*Walks over to jesters.*) Now to meet the silly jesters. How easily they are led astray! (*Taps each jester on the head just before they hop to center stage.*)

JESTERS—(*Shakespeare taps Ashlito and she hops to center stage.*) My name is Ashlito! (*Taps Addisito and then hops to center stage.*) My name is Addisito! (*Taps Charlito and then hops to center stage.*) And my name is Charlito! (*All together with arms on shoulders.*) We are the jesters for the King of Naples! We are bursting with energy all the time in order to make the King laugh. We wear bright colors to show happiness. (*Only Ashlito speaks as the other two hop behind her from side to side.*) By now you all know that we were washed ashore during the tempest. (*Elements sound effects for 30 seconds.*) Then we met up with Stephano, the rude butler, and Caliban. (*Addisito only.*) Stephano taught us to be rude and to hate the King of Naples. Caliban told us Prospero was an evil magician. (*Charlito only.*) He asked us to help him kill Prospero during the night. Ariel warned Prospero and then he spoiled our plans. (*All together*) See you later! (*All three hop back to Shakespeare and strike a pose.*)

SHAKESPEARE—(*Walks over and hand gestures to Stephano.*) Then there is that pesky Stephano, the rude butler. Stephano taught the jesters and Caliban how to be rude. (*Jesters start to laugh and hop up and down for a second. Shakespeare shakes his finger at them.*) Hey! Now cut that out! (*Jesters strike a pose again.*) Like they need any more lessons! (*Puts hand on his shoulder.*) Now, tell us your story, Stephano.

STEPHANO—(*Stephano looks at Shakespeare.*) Excu-u-use me. (*He gently takes Shakespeare's hand off his shoulder. Then Stephano strolls to center stage.*) My name is Stephano, the rude butler. I push people around and call them names. I like to shove people in the river and the mud. I even put wanted signs up for the most innocent people. I tried to make the jesters and Caliban turn into very, very rude people. We all have bad table manners. We complain about the food. We talk with food in our mouths. I am a total savage. Ha! Ha! Ha! (*Gives a sinister, loud laugh. Stumbles back to Shakespeare.*)

SHAKESPEARE—(*Returns to center stage.*) Well, there you have it!. (*Hand gestures to all of the characters*). These are some of the characters I created for my play, *The Tempest*. (*Elements sound effects for 30 seconds.*) I hope you have enjoyed them as well as I have. Thank you, for coming. (*Shakespeare waves good-bye, then strikes a pose with the other characters in the center of the stage. The elements then wave as the music plays*).

chapter 7

Creative Drama in the Classroom

by **Shannon O'Day**

rama is a natural mode of learning for children because it promotes a sense of story sequence and characterization and it forces students to become actively involved with abstract thought and language. Drama can also improve reading and critical thinking skills. Additionally, acting in the theater encourages students to work as a team because the success of a production depends on each member of the cast doing his or her share.

Gifted programs in Paulding County, GA, where I teach, are language-arts-based at the middle school level. At the elementary level they are based on thematic units. I tie both of these educational approaches together using drama. Creative drama strategies work effectively in what might appear to be overly ambitious projects.

First, I would like to discuss one innovative strategy that introduces the youngest students to the elements of drama. Young children, including gifted ones, appreciate the silly and the absurd. Humor is often mentioned as a characteristic in identifying gifted children. According to the cognitive stage theories of Jean Paiget, Lawrence Kohlberg, and Jane Loevinger and the work of Paul Ghee, children ages 4–6 enjoy and respond to clowning, silly rhyming, slapstick, and riddles. Seven- and 8-year-old children love practical jokes, and even children as old as 12 delight in knock-knock jokes and word plays. The use of humor can provide a climate for communication and can stimulate the thinking processes and learning environment (Monson, 1994).

So, how do you combine the two elements of humor and drama in a way that will engage your students' imaginations? One way is the use of melodrama. Melodrama meshes nicely with the young child's sense of humor while teaching the basics of plot and characterization and the skills of inferencing and prior knowledge. While this dramatic style can seem silly and over-the-top to adults, children, especially those in first and second grade, respond to the clowning around and the audience participation that is a part of melodrama. As an introduction to drama, I use in my classroom a series of nine melodramas, which are intended as a first step in learning how to create improvisational theater and dramatize story plots from reading material. These plays provide flexible, yet structured children's drama that teachers will feel comfortable using; they are designed for practical classroom use. Specifically, they are short and concise, with each play lasting only 5–10 minutes. This short length may be useful to teachers who have a limited amount of time to spend on dramatic activities, need a short play for a school program, and have to address the needs of new multiple-criteria legislation for gifted programs. These plays also are easy to rehearse, prepare, or augment. By spending about 1 hour per day, each play can be executed, from start to finish, in a week.

Following is a play entitled *The Rent*, the production of which is best suited for first or second graders. Teachers who use this play should follow these simple guidelines:

- Read the play with students before it is acted out.
- Do not spend more than an hour on each play session. It takes more than one session to allow students to "become" their characters, but too much rehearsal becomes tedious to gifted students who would rather create than memorize. Sessions may go as follows:

1. Read the play, choose the parts, and read it again.
2. Act out the play, getting up and moving according to the plot.
3. Tape the performance on a tape-recorder or videocamera if desired. (This helps students learn to enunciate, speak louder, and not block other actors.)
4. Act out the play with a few simple props and costumes.
5. Perform only two dress rehearsals.
6. If desired, perform for a group.

One-Act Melodrama: The Rent

Characters:
The Narrator
Annabelle
Mayflower
Grandmother
Grandfather
Mr. Snake (the villain)
Peabody (Mr. Snake's companion)
Hero
Spot the dog
The Sheriff
Children to hold signs

Plot: This is a classic melodrama about a hero, a heroine, and paying the rent.

Scenery: A simple paper backdrop of the interior of a house may be drawn.

Props: Two chairs; "Hiss," "Boo," "Ah," and "Hooray" signs; a table; a newspaper; a piggy bank; a nickel; a comb; some knitting; and items for setting the dinner table.

Setting: The living room of a small house.

NARRATOR—Annabelle is setting the table for dinner, and Mayflower is combing her hair. Grandmother is knitting while

Grandfather is reading the newspaper. Suddenly, there is a knock at the door. (*knock, knock*)

GRANDMOTHER—Annabelle, would you please answer the door. It must be the paperboy to collect the newspaper money. Tell him . . . tell him . . . to come back . . . next Tuesday.

ANNABELLE—Why do I have to answer the door? I always have to answer the door! I always have to do all the work.

MAYFLOWER—That's what younger sisters are for.

NARRATOR—Annabelle answers the door. Mr. Snake, the villain, and his helper Peabody enter.

AUDIENCE—Hiss! (*Sign holders hold up "Hiss" signs.*)

MR. SNAKE—Good evening. My name is Mr. Snake, and this is my associate, Peabody. Excuse me for intruding, but I've come to collect the rent.

MAYFLOWER—Let me check my piggy bank. (*Goes over to a large piggy bank and shakes out one nickel.*) I have a nickel. Is that enough?

PEABODY—I'm sorry, but we don't take nickels.

MAYFLOWER—Grandmother, Grandfather, do you have any money for the rent? Something other than a nickel?

GRANDMOTHER—Hummmm . . . rent money . . . where did I . . . put it?

GRANDFATHER—Quiet! Can't you see that I am reading the paper?

MR. SNAKE—Unless you can pay the rent now, I'll have to throw you out of your dingy little shack.

AUDIENCE—Boo! (*Sign holders hold up "Boo" signs.*)

MAYFLOWER—Mercy! Please don't throw us out of our dingy little shack into the cold.

AUDIENCE—Ah! (*Sign holders hold up "Ah" signs.*)

MR. SNAKE—Excuse me, but we could make a deal. Marry me, and Peabody can marry Annabelle. Then, I'll let your grandparents stay in this dingy little shack.

AUDIENCE—Hiss! (*Sign holders hold up "Hiss" sign.*)

MAYFLOWER—Never!

ANNABELLE—Never! Always never!

MR. SNAKE—Excuse me, but you really have no practical choice! You must marry me!

PEABODY—You have no money! If you don't marry us, you'll all be thrown out into the cold.

GRANDFATHER—No! I'm not cold! Can't you see I'm trying to read the paper?

MR. SNAKE—Come now and marry us!

NARRATOR—Mr. Snake and Peabody begin to chase Annabelle and Mayflower around the room.

MAYFLOWER—Help!

ANNABELLE—Help! No one ever helps me!

NARRATOR—The hero enters.

HERO—Hi, I'm a hero, so I can help you.

AUDIENCE—Hooray! (*Sign holders hold up "Hooray" signs.*)

MR. SNAKE—They must pay the rent.

HERO—I can pay the rent! I have three coupons.

PEABODY—I'm sorry, but we don't take coupons.

HERO—Then I'll call my dog, Spot, on you. Come, Spot!

AUDIENCE—Hooray! (*Sign holders hold up "Hooray" signs.*)

NARRATOR—Spot enters and chases the villains into the arms of the sheriff who is waiting at the door.

SHERIFF—I arrest you in the name of the law, and also for not paying property taxes.

AUDIENCE—Hooray! (*Sign holders hold up "Hooray" signs.*)

MR. SNAKE—(What would you say? Make up your own line.)

SHERIFF—(What would you say? Make up your own line.)

MAYFLOWER—My hero! (*Runs to Spot and hugs him.*) I'll marry you.

AUDIENCE—Ah! (*Sign holders hold up "Ah" signs.*)

ANNABELLE—You always get to marry the dog. I never get to marry the dog.

MAYFLOWER—(What would you say? Make up your own line.)

HERO—(What would you say? Make up your own line.)

SPOT—(What would you say? Make up your own line.)

GRANDMOTHER—I just remembered what I did with the rent money. I spent it on . . . Girl Scout cookies.

ANNABELLE—(What would you say? Make up your own line.)

GRANDMOTHER—(What would you say? Make up your own line.)

GRANDFATHER—(What would you say? Make up your own line.)

NARRATOR—(What would you say? Make up your own line.)

SIGN HOLDERS—(What sign would you hold up? You choose.)

You will notice that the last key lines of the play are left blank, thus enabling students to supply their own ending. Students may write their last lines in the scripts and do not need to memorize them. However, since the play is short, it does lend itself to easy memorization. Because students may be hesitant about making up their own lines, remember to give them time to think them up. This type of exercise in creative thought requires a period of reflection.

Keep in mind that you can aid your students with their endings. Martin Kimeldorf (1994) noted that children often have a difficult time deciding on appropriate conclusions for plays. They introduce a new character or situation that is illogical and contrived. However, Kimeldorf suggested that you can use this opportunity to explain the fundamentals for constructing a believable storyline. Explain that new characters or a new twist in the plot cannot be introduced suddenly at the end of a story. In this way, students learn about plot and how it relates to the dramatic experience.

More Advanced Productions

Once students have mastered the rudiments of plot, characterization, and, of course, acting, they can move on to bigger, more complicated productions. My second and third graders have successfully tackled *Julius Caesar*, while fourth and fifth graders have produced a Japanese version of scenes from *A Midsummer Night's Dream*. These ambitious Shakespearean productions came about because my second and third graders were involved in a unit on ancient Rome and the fourth and fifth graders were studying Japan. This allowed me to introduce Shakespeare into the various themes and still remain within each unit's topic.

My second and third graders studied the life of Julius Caesar and then read the scene in Shakespeare's play in which Mark Antony speaks over Caesar's body. The students did not need to read the entire Shakespearean play because we were exploring the issue of how Mark Antony used language and rhetoric to sway people to his side. My students were especially struck by Antony's use of flattery, for example, the constant use of the phrase "honorable men." After studying this scene, I then had my students condense this section and write the scene so that it would make sense to their contemporary audience, but still retain its original meaning. This rewriting served as a comprehension check as my students actively showed me that they understood Shakespeare's ideas by putting them in their own words. They could not just recite memorized lines and stay at the received knowledge level. They had to do some work at the constructed knowledge level.

Students at the fourth- and fifth-grade level also had to work at the constructed knowledge level. They were studying Japan, but we needed to work in a Shakespearean production theme. The seventh grade was in the process of acting out one of its favorite scenes from *A Midsummer Nights Dream*. Hence, the fourth and fifth graders chose to act out the same scene, but with a Japanese interpretation. Would the same theme work in another culture and a different language? As we were limited by time and a lack of Japanese, we, like Shakespeare, created our own words (Shakespeare created 2,000 words that he added to the English language). Actually we used the names of Tokyo subway stations for play dialogue. Once again, Shakespeare's ideas proved universal because the play made just as much sense performed in a Japanese mode as it does in its English one. Students also learned, in an active sense, that it is not what you say, but how you say it.

Both of these productions proved that creative drama not only aids in reading comprehension, but it also can be an effective way of exploring other subjects and topics. Students at the Herschel Jones Middle School in Paulding County, GA, performed "The Mad Hatter's Tea Party," a scene from *Alice in Wonderland*, as part of a sociology activity. My seventh graders felt that the theme of the book was that people, especially adolescents, will do anything to try to fit in with their peers. Using creative drama, the class decided to really test its ideas. It chose "The Mad Hatter's Tea Party" as a good example of Alice trying to fit into a particularly awkward situation. They wrote this scene in their own words, but left out the part of Alice. Instead, as part of their sociology experiment, other students and adults would be asked to participate in this play. My seventh-grade students wrote out a checklist that measured the comfort level and reported the reactions of subjects placed in the situation of attending the Mad Hatter's tea party. The qualitative study looked at the differences in gender and age. There were 20 subjects who were randomly chosen. Hypotheses about gender and age were tested, and the theme of *Alice in Wonderland* was found to hold true, but not quite in the manner predicted. The experiment opened a few more doors on questions of quantitative versus qualitative analysis and the impact of culture and gender bias. Once again, creative drama proved a valuable tool in the learning process.

One other activity that uses creative drama to both entertain and educate is our yearly fundraiser. Students, after completing the plays in the nine-play melodrama series, write their own plays, such as the Shakespearean interpretations, and present them to the community at large. The plays are staged in the form of a dinner theater, and the whole community participates. The result is a growth in learning for students, parents, and the larger community. In this instance and in many others, creative drama provides one of the greatest of all educational motivations: meaningful fun.

References

Kimeldorf, M. (1994). *Exciting writing, successful speaking: Activities to make language come alive in the classroom.* Minneapolis, MN: Free Spirit.

Monson, J. (1994). Getting serious about humor: Using humor with students can lead to creative endeavors. *Gifted Child Today, 17*(5), 14–17, 40–41.

Instructional Strategies for Teaching Students Gifted in English/ Language Arts

chapter 8

Adventures With Words

*storytelling as language experience
for gifted learners*

by **Sharon Black**

> The music guided her through the moon-
> less night and although she was exhausted,
> she kept on paddling. She was getting near
> to Mokoia but the cold water had chilled
> her to the bone and she began to feel very
> weak. The music sounded faint now but
> all the same it gave her courage to press on.
> Suddenly she felt as if she might be within
> shouting distance of the Island. She put a
> foot down in the water and touched some
> waving weed. A minute later she felt solid
> land and climbed, stiffly, out of the water.
> (Te Kanawa, 1989, p. 40)

*T*his Maori tale, repeated to her often in her childhood, was recalled by opera singer Kiri Te Kanawa
many years and half a world away:

> As a child I used to go [to Lake Rotorua]
> quite often and watch the silver moon
> shining over the water. It never seemed to
> be a rough or difficult lake—always rip-

pling. Seeing the island of Mokoia in the middle of it I always picture Hinemoa swimming to her hero, her warrior, Tutaneki, and I always imagine her as a kind of fairy princess. (Te Kanawa, 1989, p. 40)

As a gifted-child-turned-adult, Te Kanawa used words that recall the vivid visual, tactile, and kinesthetic details that drew her imaginatively into Hinemoa's world, both in retelling the story and in recalling her reaction to it. Her language still flows with the rhythm of the Maori storytellers. The heritage she received from them includes not only gods, demigods, heroes, kings, princesses, fairies, and monsters, but the rhythmic language and vivid imagery with which they were portrayed.

Rhythmic language and vivid imagery can be the heritage of all children, particularly those who are of high ability. Story listening and storytelling are natural media for gifted children, who tend to be both sensitive to language and quick to pick up on imaginative possibilities.

As Renzulli (1992) has stressed, "All cognitive behavior is enhanced as a function of the degree of interest that is present . . . wherever that cognitive behavior may be on the continuum from basic skill learning to higher levels of creative productivity" (p. 173). The excitement and drama of storytelling provides a context that holds students' attention (Cooter, 1991). In this context, students experience the power of language in unique and captivating ways. Experienced classroom storyteller Olga Nelson (1989) commented that the storytelling experience "gives an appropriate example of how language can be used to make the ordinary unique" with a "wonderful interplay of language, experience, and story" (p. 389). And, the skills and capabilities developed in both language and imagination are on the highest levels of both basic usefulness and creative productivity.

Through listening to stories, students experience the musical and pictorial magic of language; through creating and sharing their own narratives, they learn how this magic can be used to express the stories, feelings, and images in their own creative minds. Polynesian stories will be used as illustrations in this chapter, as the ancient cultures, characters, and narratives are not well known and children must rely on language and imagination in receiving them. However, it is recommended that stories from a variety of nationalities, cultures, and ethnic groups be included in the ongoing use of storytelling in the classroom. The techniques and activities suggested here can be used in general classrooms or gifted pull-out programs; most can be easily adapted for home use, as well.

Story Listening

After listening to a professional storyteller, a 9-year-old child wrote this poem:

The boring words—
I look at them dragging their feet
But when the exciting marvelous words
Jump out, I dance and sing with them.
(cited in Colwell, 1980)

For a language-sensitive child, words do dance and sing. They sing as the child listens to the tone, the rhythm, the "full range of sounds and silences" (Barton, 1986) the words create. They dance as they convey to the child's imagination the sensory stimuli that allow him or her to "perceive the ordinary world with an 'uncommon eye,'" storing impressions from the senses, even crossing between senses to see what is heard and touch what is seen (Khatena, 1979, p. 735).

When the story is told, rather than read, neither the physical barrier of the book nor the imaginative barrier of illustrations come between the face, voice, and words of the teller and the attention and imagination of the listener. In a carefully planned story listening experience, children share with the storyteller both the music of language and the sensory imagery that language can convey.

Sharing the Music of Language

When a teacher begins a classroom experience with "a certain chief who lived on the island of Oahu in the very misty memory of long, long ago" (Westervelt, 1964, p. 65), the language itself draws children into a story. A storytelling session, like a concert, is a performance; the artist expresses the content through sound, and the audience receives it through the auditory sense. Bob Barton (1986), who has had many years of successful storytelling experiences, explained that "the sound and rhythm of the words are often all part of the meaning" (p. 45).

Just as a child's ear for music is trained and strengthened by listening to music, a child's ear for language is strengthened and trained through listening to language (see Colwell, 1980). The storytelling experience is one of the most effective ways to help children respond to its rhythm and beauty (Livo & Reitz, 1986). Barton (1986) referred to a distinctive sound for each story, "the special aura that story radiates" (p. 56). Specific sounds, he commented, do or do not "belong" to that story (p. 56). Pacing, pauses, intonation, and even mimicry can be effective (Huntsman, 1990).

Distinctive sounds and sound differences can be easily perceived when ethnic or multicultural stories are used. For example, Polynesian languages are smooth and flowing, as each syllable and each word ends with a vowel, and two consonants are never used in succession without a vowel between them. When Polynesian names are used in a story, they seem to glide as they are pronounced: *Kaili-lau-o-kekoa*, *Ku-leo-nui*, *Mu-lei-ula*, *Kaanaelike*, or *Kamalama*. The first man, according to Hawaiian legend, was *Wela-ahi-lani-nui* (The Great Heaven Burning Hot), and the first woman was *Ke-aka-huli-lani* (The-Heaven-Changed-Shadow). A storyteller need not be afraid of Polynesian names; they are pronounced just as they are spelled, since written language was brought to the islands and superimposed on an already well-developed oral tongue. All one needs to remember is to emphasize the vowels. The storyteller can talk about the sound of Polynesian words before beginning the story and invite the children to pronounce the names with him or her as they occur. Even in translation, the names are musical and flowing, as they involve multiple expressive words: "Listen to the Heavenly Voice," "The Covering of the Mekoa Leaf," "Child Nourished by the Gods," "Mu With the Red Garland" (Names taken from legends recorded in Rice, 1977; Westervelt, 1964).

A storyteller may use patterns of language structure and imagery, as well as vocabulary, in telling a story, thus introducing children to the characteristic rhythms and melodies these patterns create (Baker & Greene, 1987). Since Polynesian languages developed exclusively in oral form, there are few abstract words; thus, feelings and emotions are often expressed figuratively, especially in personification. The personified item is usually in the subject position, most often near the beginning of the sentence. For example, in "Ulukaa, The Rolling Island," when a king is washed up on the shore of a floating island, "hunger whispered to him," and "the king did as hunger bade him." When he marries the beautiful princess of the island, he exclaims, "Now great happiness dwells with us." When he dreams of his parents' heartbreak over his reported death, he is not told "they aren't sleeping well," but "sleep comes not often to them;" in fact, "three times the same dream came to him" and "hourly this dream, like an image, haunted him" (Rice, 1977, pp. 20–26). There is a rhythm to this personification that a storyteller can learn and easily recall. It isn't necessary to memorize the story; by repeating the sentences a number of times, listening for the rhythm and becoming accustomed to the pattern, the storyteller will sense naturally where and how these patterns of meaning and expression should be used.

Where gifted children are generally sensitive to the suggestibility of language, both in sound and in figurative use, the storyteller could make brief comments describing these sound and structure patterns before telling the story, much as a music teacher might talk about style and introduce major themes from a piece of music before playing an orchestral recording. The flow of the words in the story should not be interrupted to explain features of the language. Many storytellers have their listeners repeat and practice key ethnic or native language words before the story begins and then participate by calling the words out or chanting them at specific places during the performance.

Sharing the Imagery of Language

A Hawaiian legend describes the destruction of a tree beloved to the goddess Haumea—"'the tree of changing leaves' with two flowers, one kind singing sharply, and the other singing from time to time":

That night a fierce and mighty storm came down from the mountains. Blood-red were the streams of water pouring down into the valleys. During twenty nights and twenty days the angry rain punished the land. . . . The river was more than a rushing torrent. It built up hills and dug ravines. It hurled its mighty waves against the wall inside which the tree stood. It crushed the wall, scattered the stones, and bore the tree down one of the deep ravines. . . .

The body of the tree rolled back and forth along the beach near the four waters, and was wrapped in the refuse of the sea. (Westervelt, 1964, pp. 25–26)

As they experience the way language sounds, children who listen to stories also experience the way language can make them see and feel. It is this blending of auditory and visual capabilities of language that gives storytelling its power; and, in turn, the power of the aesthetic and emotional experience brings to linguistically sensitive children an understanding of the properties of language as a medium. As Sasser and Zorena (1991) expressed it, gifted children who listen to stories experience "the originality and color" of speech.

Bob Barton (1986), a storyteller who performs often for groups of school children, knew he had succeeded when he received a letter from a kindergarten class that told him, "You said the words that helped us think the pictures" (p. 8). In fact, many experienced storytellers comment that the story should enter the listeners' minds as a series of moving pictures (Barton; Breneman & Breneman, 1983), and that the storyteller can best prepare by learning the story, not as a series of words to recall, but as a sequence of pictures to describe (Cooter, 1991). The storytelling/story listening experience is often referred to as an act of cocreation between the teller and the audience (Baker & Greene, 1987; Breneman & Breneman; Nelson, 1989). Language is the medium by which the pictures are conveyed, and well-chosen language allows the listeners to "actualize the story in their [own] minds" (Nelson, p. 386).

The medium of language contains many raw materials the storyteller can use to invite the cocreation of his or her pictures. Carefully chosen adjectives and adverbs can convey multifaceted pictures; but, it is important to remember that nouns and verbs are the heart of the sentence. Vivid and specific verbs convey visual and occasionally auditory and kinesthetic information. Many words, especially nouns, convey emotions along with the more objective material. Color, texture, taste, smell, and even temperature are involved in sharing adventures and experiences (Chambers, 1977). In addition to the traditional senses, story-tellers might consider equilibrium (balance; see Breneman & Breneman, 1983), especially in stories that involve sailing or rowing, struggling physically with an adversary, walking or run-ning in unfamiliar places, or lifting or carrying heavy objects. It is also important to use vivid words that convey organic sensa-tions such as dizziness, hunger, or pain, along with specific words that communicate emotional reactions such as forebod-ing, surprise, guilt, or anger (see Breneman & Breneman).

Sensory experiences expressed by words are enhanced when those words state or imply a comparison. Analogy adds richness and emotion to any description. Through carefully chosen analogies, a storyteller brings intangible and elusive elements into focus quickly and vividly. As Khatena (1984) expressed it, a "familiar situation to which the thought-feeling complex can be related . . . a process of making the strange familiar or the familiar strange" (pp. 154–155; see also Gordon, 1961; Gowan, 1979). Remembering well-chosen analogies helps a storyteller recall important aspects of the story, and it enhances the lan-guage experience for the children. In Hawaiian legends and folklore, people and places are often compared to natural phe-nomena. For example, in describing the mother of the hero Kana, the storyteller notes, "Her skin was like the sun as it rises, or like the feather of the mamo" (Rice, 1977, p. 107). Another beauty, Kaili-lau-o-kekoa, has cheeks that "glowed like the rising sun" (Rice, p. 117). The goddess Papa is described as "a beauti-ful woman whose skin shone like polished dark ivory through the flowers and vines and leaves which were the only clothes she knew" (Westervelt, 1964, p. 29).

After the children have heard the story uninterrupted so that they can respond to the power of the language experience, selected passages might be retold. Torrance (1979) recom-mended repetition of passages one time through strictly for lis-tening and spontaneous response, another specifically for mental pictures, and possibly another for varying personal interpretations. Where gifted children are capable of finding within their language experiences raw material for their own future storytelling and writing, multiple viewing and reexamining could be particularly significant.

Storytelling

This ability to find models in the expression of others makes it essential that gifted children's experience in storytelling not be limited to listening. As listeners, they cocreate stories told by others, and they must complete the experience by sharing their own stories from the teller's position. Because storytelling groups will vary from young to more mature, from homogeneous to heterogeneous, from single grade to multiage, the storyteller should develop a repertoire comprising a wide variety of involvement and sharing activities. Such activities should include opportunities for sharing personal expression in a number of modalities, for sharing the joy and excitement of using language creatively, and for new forms of thought and expression generated by the story listening experiences.

Sharing Personal Expression

In discussing the needs of today's gifted children, Roberto Assagioli (1987) suggested:

> Imagination is of great importance in human life and has more influence than is generally recognized; therefore it should receive particular attention. The training should include exercises of visualization, creative imagination etc., so that young people will gradually learn how to control and rightly use this precious function. (p. 54)

As part of their storytelling participation, gifted children need to give expression to the imaginative impulses that are generated as they listen to stories.

A storytelling circle is an authentic cultural experience that provides such participation opportunities, allowing for variation in ages, ability levels, and dominant and preferred modes of expression. Historically and currently, oral literature has been created and performed in such circles in cultures all over the world. In areas such as the Polynesian islands, dances and songs accompany the stories. Puppetry and other forms of creative dramatics can be part of these gatherings, as well.

Creating oral stories is a natural form of expression for young children's creativity, as they are freed from the necessity of having to write legibly, spell words correctly, or obey other conventions of writing. The instant feedback they receive from the listeners helps them develop a sense of audience; it also provides a subtle reality check for their communication skills. Brief nature fables, common to a variety of cultures, are simple and fairly easy for young children to create after they have listened to a few examples. Each child could bring from home a natural object such as an interesting stone, flower, leaf, or bird's nest. Then, in turn, each could show the object and tell the story, having thought out a basic story outline in advance. Children who are less verbally able or less confident than their classmates could practice with their parents in advance.

For children who have entered the phase of the middle elementary years where they enjoy hero stories, a series of stories could be shared by the teacher or guest storyteller centered around a mythic hero, such as Maui of the Polynesians, Loki of the Scandinavians, or Hermes of the Greeks. Then, the children could each add an adventure from their own imaginations. Or, they could create their own class hero for whom each could contribute an adventure. Another variation would be to have each child invent his own personalized hero to star in a new heroic tale. Thus, the stories told in the circle could be created within as much or as little structure as the teacher considers ideal for the specific group.

Children whose talent areas include capabilities other than verbal skills can work with additional modalities to enhance the language experience of the story circle. Drawings or other visual creations are a natural addition, particularly if the children are telling monster tales or other stories in which new kinds of creatures or supernatural beings are invented. For example, in the Maori lore of New Zealand, the *taniwha*, or human-eating monster, took his shape from the fears of the people. Thus, many noted taniwhas were shaped like lizards, as the ancient Maori had a cultural fear of lizards; however, one of the best-known taniwhas of people who lived near the sea was shaped like a giant sea monster (Anderson, 1928). Children could prepare for the storytelling circle by creating their own taniwhas, with shapes influenced by their own fears. These creations could be drawn, painted, or finger-painted, or they could be created as three-dimensional clay figures or collages. Finding words to describe their visual creations will stimulate the children's ability to use sensory descriptive language.

Children with talents in music could create and perform songs as part of their participation in the storytelling circle. Instrumental music and dance could be invited, performed either individually or in groups to enhance the effects of the stories. Blending the words with the musical and kinesthetic representations makes the children more aware of the cross-sensory capabilities of language. Inclusion of creative drama or simple puppet performances utilizes an additional dimension of language by requiring students to vary their word choice to represent both characterization and basic narrative action.

Sharing the Joy of Language

Regardless of the complexity of the stories or the addition of other talent modalities, the medium of storytelling is language, and the dominant product is language development. Professional storyteller Dewey Chambers (1977) commented that, through storytelling, children "experience living language, a language that communicates at a level above and beyond that of everyday usage" (p. 45). He explained that "living words can create a world, pose and solve problems, influence emotions, and create images" (p. 45). Gifted children need opportunities to create and share their own worlds, to pose and solve problems that enter their own minds. With a little ingenuity from the teacher, such experiences can become available.

Experienced storytellers Livo and Reitz (1986) suggested that awareness and enjoyment of language can begin with something as simple as riddles and humorous wordplay. Key words from stories the children have heard can generate language games. For example, a professional storyteller who was using ethnic Jewish stories had a multiage group of children enthralled with what they could do with the world *schlemiel* (D. Richin, personal observation, July 1997).

Keeping the informal atmosphere in which individuality and humor are encouraged, creating simple stories centered around group interaction is a logical next step. As Torrance (1965) has pointed out, creative children need to look for relationships, find new and interesting combinations, and synthesize things that may seem unrelated into new products. Creating new adventures for a favorite character in a story they have already enjoyed (particularly a minor character) allows for new views and combinations of material the group holds in common. Or the children could add a new character to a previously enjoyed adventure (a rival warrior just as handsome as the original chief's son, a fourth brother questing after the king's daughter, a jealous sister for the princess). Secondary English teacher W.W. West (1980) suggested giving students five objects to develop into a story. If a group had been listening to folk tales from Polynesia, they might be given a fishing hook, a coconut, a braided mat, a stone, and an egg. As these items are common in the lives of Polynesians, they could generate stories of the natural or supernatural, distant past or present day, chiefs and kings or common people. The teacher could encourage and reinforce variety in the creations, as well as vividness and originality in language. For groups that are younger, multiage, or widely varied in language ability, descriptive words for the objects could be brainstormed to get the children thinking in terms of vivid language, while scaffolding could be provided for those who need it.

For more formal storytelling experiences—for which stories are more painstakingly created and possibly performed for a wider audience—more time, less structure, and fewer distractions would be desirable. Gowan (1979) commented that students' abilities to generate creative, sensory imagery is increased by reducing outside sensory input and calming "internal verbal chatter" (p. 2). Although the external and internal chatter generated by the informal group activities is helpful in promoting initial enthusiasm and stockpiling raw materials, if students are going to create pieces that will represent their talents and allow them to perform, then they will need personal time and possibly space. Sasser and Zorena (1991) advised that performance is an important aspect of the storytelling experience, that it adds "an element of drama (literally, as well as emotionally)" (p. 44). Thus, it heightens children's personal involvement in the activities and their awareness of language use.

Sharing New Styles of Thought and Expression

Once children are finding words to express creatively feelings and sensations, as well as happenings, a logical next step is to develop those sensations and impressions into analogies. According to Khatena (1978) in his writings concerning language and giftedness, analogical thinking is "one of the most potent creative energy sources," and an individual who is able to think in terms of analogies "stands an excellent chance at being creative, inventive, and a good problem solver" (p. 83). Davis (1989) agreed, commenting that "perhaps the most common and widely used idea-finding technique is deliberate analogical thinking" (p. 83).

Khatena's (1973) studies have shown that analogies come naturally to gifted children. By examining analogies made by children of varying ages, he found that young children (ages 8–9) make simple direct analogies more frequently than do older children, but older children (ages 12–13) are more inclined to develop their analogies to a complex level. Khatena (1984) suggested that teachers give students a word pool from which they can choose words on which they want to base original analogies. If the words in the pool happen to be key words that have been involved in a storytelling experience, the children already have sensations and associations linked to them, which makes analogies an easy and natural step forward.

Additional activities related to story listening and storytelling experiences can extend the natural interest of the stories into analogy motivation. Because the early Polynesian people lived close to nature and used nature to define their daily thoughts and activities, their stories are filled with analogies. In many stories, the analogy is the center of the tale. Take, for example, the Samoan legend of the two-mouthed sea cucumber. During a battle between the birds and the fish, the sea cucumber cheers enthusiastically for the birds when they are winning and tells them the strategies the fish are planning to use. But, when the fish change their strategies and begin to drive the birds back into the bush, the sea cucumber immediately begins to cheer for the fish. Both the birds and the fish say that the sea cucumber has two mouths—one to talk to the birds and the other to talk to the fish—so he cannot be trusted. The sea cucumber is condemned to live only in shallow places where he can be easily watched, and his two mouths can do little harm (Steubel, Kraemer, & Herman, 1995). Even the youngest children can look at a picture of a sea cucumber and see that it does not really have two mouths. This leads naturally into a discussion of what analogies are and why they are effective in helping people understand and remember abstract ideas such as loyalty and trust.

To reinforce the concept of using the familiar to explore the abstract, the teacher could bring a box or basket of objects and allow each child to choose something to develop into an analogy. For greater variety, a set of pictures of sea creatures, animals, plants, or other objects could be used in a game in which children see how many analogies they can generate individually, in small groups, or as a class. If stories from a particular culture are being told as examples, pictures of nature or artifacts related specifically to that culture could be used. For example, a picture of the peninsula on the Island of Oahu—a land and rock formation shaped like a turtle with just the tip of the tail touching the larger island—could generate a variety of interesting analogies.

Puppets might be furnished by the teacher or created by the children themselves to act as voices for analogies, encouraging children to develop their analogies in more complex directions and in greater detail. Puppets could become the tellers of "teaching stories," like that of the sea cucumber; many children tend to experiment more with language and with innovative ideas under the "safety" of an imaginative persona.

Conclusion

Storyteller Bob Barton (1986) insisted that "Stories are wonderful meeting places" (p. 8). Stories furnish many significant encounters for children with special gifts and talents. As they look into the eyes of a storyteller and hear his or her voice using language to create the world of a story, children encounter the musical and pictorial qualities of language that is used not merely as a daily necessity, but as an art. Khatena (1984) referred to it as "the language of discovery." With no physical pictures, children learn that language can create mental pictures through which they can explore new worlds and experience new cultures. As they create and share their own stories, children learn to use the properties of language to create new worlds and explore the resources of their own minds. As they use such creative language, "like artists in the act of painting, they give organization and meaning to these images" (Khatena, p. 156). Particular attention should be paid to "how they depict their world, what details they include, the choices they make of colors, the style they choose and the extent to which they allow their emotions to become involved" as concerned with "creative energizing forces at work" (p. 156). In the process, they encounter their own imaginative potential, the fun involved in experimenting and playing with language, and the fascination of extending language play into creative expressions such as analogies. Through listening to stories and creating and telling their own, gifted and creative children meet and explore, through language, both external and internal worlds.

References

Anderson, J. C. (1928). *Myths and legends of the Polynesians.* New York: Farrar & Rinehart.

Assagioli, R. (1987). The education of gifted and highly gifted children. *Gifted Education International, 5*, 52–56.

Baker, A., & Greene, E. (1987). *Storytelling: Art and technique* (2nd ed.). London: Bowker.

Barton, B. (1986). *Tell me another: Storytelling and reading aloud at home, at school, and in the community.* Portsmouth, NH: Heinemann.

Breneman, L. N., & Breneman, B. (1983). *Once upon a time: A storytelling handbook.* Chicago: Nelson Hall.

Chambers, D. W. (1977). *The oral tradition: Storytelling and creative drama* (2nd ed.). Dubuque, IA: Brown.

Colwell, E. (1980). *Storytelling.* London: The Bodley Head Ltd.

Cooter, R. B. (1991). Storytelling in the language arts classroom. *Reading Research and Instruction, 30*(2), 71–76.

Davis, G. A. (1989). Objectives and activities for teaching creative thinking. *Gifted Child Quarterly, 33*, 81–83.

Gordon, W. J. J. (1961). *Synectics: The development of creative capacity.* New York: Harper and Row.

Gowan, J. C. (1979). The production of creativity through right hemisphere imagery. *Journal of Creative Behavior, 13*(1), 39–51.

Huntsman, J. (1990). Fiction, fact, and imagination: A Tokelau narrative. *Oral Tradition, 5*, 283–315.

Khatena, J. (1973). Imagination imagery of children and the production of analogy. *Gifted Child Quarterly, 17*, 98–102.

Khatena, J. (1978). *The creatively gifted child: Suggestions for parents and teachers.* New York: Vintage Press.

Khatena, J. (1979). The nature of imagery in the visual and performing arts. *Gifted Child Quarterly, 23*, 735–747.

Khatena, J. (1984). *Imagery and creative imagination.* Buffalo, NY: Bearly Ltd.

Livo, N. S., & Reitz, S. A. (1986). *Storytelling: Process and practice.* Littleton, CO: Libraries Unlimited.

Nelson, O. (1989). Storytelling: Language experience for meaning making. *The Reading Teacher, 42*, 386–390.

Renzulli, J. S. (1992). General theory for the development of creative productivity through the pursuit of ideal acts of learning. *Gifted Child Quarterly, 36*, 170–182.

Rice, W. H. (Ed. & Trans.). (1977). *Hawaiian legends.* Honolulu: Bishop Museum Press.

Sasser, E., & Zorena, N. (1991). Storytelling as an adjunct to writing: Experiences with gifted students. *Teaching Exceptional Children, 23*(2), 44–45.

Steubel, C., Kraemer, A., & Herman, B. (Eds. & Trans.). (1995). *Tala o le vavau: The myths, customs, and legends of old Samoa.* Auckland, New Zealand: Pasifika Press.

Te Kanawa, K. (1989). *Land of the long white cloud: Maori myths, tales, and legends.* New York: Arcade.

Torrance, E. P. (1965). *Gifted children in the classroom.* New York: Macmillan.

Torrance, E. P. (1979). An instructional model for enhancing incubation. *Journal of Creative Behavior, 13*, 23–34.

West, W. W. (1980). *Teaching the gifted and talented in the English classroom.* Washington, DC: National Education Association.

Westervelt, W. D. (1964). *Hawaiian legends of old Honolulu.* Rutland, VT: Tuttle.

chapter 9

Using the Literary Masters to Inspire Expression in Gifted Students

by **Sheila R. Albers, Christa M. Martin,** *and* **Deidra M. Gammill**

hroughout history, gifted writers have enriched the human experience with the power and beauty of words. These literary masters enlighten us to universal truths, expand our minds to new ideas and visions, and challenge us to advance civilization. Exposing gifted students to the vast realm of important literature can inspire them to find their own voices and attain personal growth while making contributions to their culture. Their natural inclination to explore ideas and manipulate linguistic expressions endows gifted children with the potential to become great writers (Fraser, 2003; Kauffman & Gentile, 2002; Renzulli, Smith, White, Callahan, Hartman, & Westberg 2002).

Unfortunately, little emphasis is placed on writing instruction in both general and gifted education. In fact, the National Commission on Writing in America's Schools and Colleges (2003) reported that only 1 in 4 students scored "proficient" on federal writing tests. Teachers can increase the emphasis on writing instruction in their own classrooms by providing more opportunities for students to express themselves in meaningful ways. Research has long supported the effectiveness of teaching written expression in conjunction with reading instruction (e.g., Cixous, 1990; Cordon, 2000; DeFord, 1981; Flower, 1990; Lee, 2000; Stotsky, 1983). Immersion in prominent works combined with motivating writing instruction can bridge the gap between natural ability and the production of quality written expression.

This article provides suggested writing activities that are embedded in the study of literature. These activities were designed for the unique characteristics of gifted students.

Characteristics of Gifted Students

Gifted students possess cognitive and linguistic abilities that make them good candidates for advanced writing instruction. Specifically, these students have a highly developed capacity for language expression, advanced perceptive ability (Renzulli et al., 2002), and the aptitude to generate unique responses (Fraser, 2003). Additionally, gifted students delight in the world of language, understand hidden meanings and inferences, and they possess an advanced sense of humor (Renzulli et al.; VanTassel-Baska, 2003).

With these characteristics in mind, educators have identified ways to cultivate and enhance creativity. In general, gifted students need exposure to a broad range of concepts and contexts, novel products, and in-depth cultural material (Fasko, 2000/2001; Kline, 2000; VanTassel-Baska, 1989). In conjunction with exposure, gifted students need encouragement and freedom to pursue and deeply explore their interests independently. This combination of exposure, encouragement, and freedom helps gifted students construct their own beliefs and discover what they need to say (VanTassel-Baska, 2003).

By studying the literary masters—their works, influences, and personal lives—gifted students can develop advanced perspective and original thought.

Effective originality depends first of all upon sound and exhaustive knowledge of what the course of preceding events has been. To take their unique places in civilized society, it would seem therefore that the intellectually gifted need especially to know what the evolution of culture has been. (Hollingworth, 1938, p. 297)

With this statement as a guiding principle, we suggest several activities that will enhance and expand gifted students' knowledge of literary history and guide them in the creation of original written expression. These activities are designed for students in grades 8–12, although they can be easily adapted for younger children.

Independent Exploration

An important goal of education is to empower students to become independent learners. Gifted students begin independent learning during early childhood, and, later in life, they consider themselves primarily self-taught. These students often study a topic of interest extensively and become immersed in their work (Fasko, 2000/2001; VanTassel-Baska, 2003). Teachers can promote and encourage this self-motivation by providing a variety of choices for students to explore. Instead of directly teaching the history and substance of literature, teachers can present general categories of how literature might be organized and direct students to select an area for exploration. Appendices A, B, and C are examples of how literature can be categorized. They were designed for teachers to use as a structural framework to help students understand the big picture of literature. For example, Appendix A shows examples of literary masters categorized by period and culture. Using this matrix, teachers can direct students to the following independent research and writing assignments.

- Select one author from the matrix for biographical study. Describe major events in the author's life and his or her major works. Discuss how the author's personal experiences may have influenced his or her writing. Additionally, discuss how you think the author's time period and culture influenced his or her work.

- Select from the matrix a few authors from one time period and culture to compare and contrast. For example, in Greek culture through the 1st century A.D., how were the lives and works of Homer, Aesop, Sophocles, and Euripides similar and different? What aspects of ancient Greek culture were likely to influence each of those authors?

- Select one culture from the matrix and research how its literature evolved from the beginning to present. For example, what was going on in North America in the 17th century that set the stage for authors like Cotton Mather and Anne Bradstreet? What was going on in North America in the 18th century that influenced the work of Phyllis Wheatly and Thomas Paine? Students may continue this exploration up through the 20th century, looking at cultural influences on such authors as F. Scott Fitzgerald and Alice Walker.

- Select one period from the matrix and research literary masters from around the world who lived during that time. Describe the relationship between those authors and the historical events that may have shaped their writing. For example, the 19th century produced writers like Karl Marx in the Germanic culture, Victor Hugo in the French culture, Leo Tolstoy in the Slavic culture, and Jane Austin in the English culture. What world events might have inspired or influenced these famous authors?

Exploration of literary masters by time and place will provide students with a broad context within which they can connect new learning. Additionally, this process is likely to help students identify specific authors or literature they are inspired to read. For example, an investigation of the early 20th century (e.g., World War I, the Depression, World War II, the beginnings of the Cold War) may inspire students to read George Orwell's Nineteen Eighty-Four, John Stein-beck's The Grapes of Wrath, Pearl S. Buck's The Good Earth, or Richard Wright's

Native Son. The individual experiences of authors may also interest students to read their works. For example, a student might be inspired to read Crime and Punishment upon discovering that its author, Fyodor Dostoevsky, wrote it after he was released from 19 years of imprisonment and exile for alleged political crimes against the Russian czar. Whatever the source of inspiration, students should be encouraged to select a piece of literature they would like to read. A student's chosen piece of writing can begin to serve as a connecting link to other works of interest and to his or her knowledge about literature in general. The following section describes group activities that originate from students' individually selected pieces of literature.

Cooperative Learning

Research indicates that effective instruction for gifted students must be flexible, stimulating, and challenging (Fasko, 2000/2001; Kline, 2000). Additionally, in order to promote social skill development, educators recommend providing opportunities for gifted students to work with peers (Fasko). The independent exploration activities in the section above were designed to provide students with direction for in depth study, while the following cooperative learning activities provide opportunities for students to work together and teach one another what they have learned independently.

• Have the students select a piece of literature to read. Tell them that prior to reading the selection that they need to research the author and events from the time period when the work was published. Direct students to write a critical analysis of the book in the context of its place in history. What events influenced this literature? What was the author trying to tell us? For example, the Spanish civil war started in 1937, and Ernest Hemmingway became involved with Spain's loyalist army. His novel For Whom the Bell Tolls tells the story of an American fighting the fascist forces in Spain. Hemmingway centralizes the conflict of war on one man. He is saying that every war is a crisis we all share, and the death of one individual diminishes the rest of us. Students should elaborate on their analyses and provide references from the

literature to support their viewpoints. Once this writing assignment is complete, the students will teach their piece of literature
to their peers in cooperative learning groups.

• After the students have shared their literature with their
cooperative learning groups, each group should attempt to identify the common threads across the selected works. Students can
discuss and record how their selected readings are similar to one
another in terms of theme, mood, characters, plot, setting, style,
or any other aspect they wish to explore. For example, the common thread might be that the protagonist experiences personal
isolation (e.g., Herman Melville's Moby Dick, Franz Kafka's
Metamorphosis, Jean Paul Sartre's Nausea, Willa Cather's Death
Comes for the Archbishop) or overcomes great obstacles (e.g.,
John Bunyan's The Pilgrim's Progress, Maya Angelou's I Know
Why the Caged Bird Sings, Victor Hugo's Les Misérables).
Once the common thread is identified, the cooperative learning
groups will have a starting point for preparing a cohesive class
presentation. Cooperative groups should be encouraged to build
whole-class discussion into their presentations.

• Another cooperative learning activity involves groups selecting and exploring representative authors of one type of literature. Examples of types of literature are listed in Appendix B.
The team members will discuss which type of literature they
would like to investigate, the particular works they would like to
read, and who will read which work. They may choose from the
examples listed in Appendix B, or they may select other works
or categories. This arrangement allows for a variety of directions
for study. For example, Team I selected "Romanticism," and
each team member selected one of the following works to read:
Daniel Defoe's Robinson Crusoe, James Fenimore Cooper's The
Last of the Mohicans, Edgar Allen Poe's The Fall of the House
of Usher, and Mark Twain's The Adventures of Tom Sawyer.
Based on their readings and discussion, the group will collaboratively define and write what "Romanticism" means and how
each work illustrates the team's definition. Students should be
encouraged to investigate other sources and critical analyses to
help shape their definitions. The final product of this activity is
a class presentation.

- Team members may also read and examine one piece of literature and discuss their individual interpretations. They may then present their interpretations to their classmates in the form of a panel discussion or debate. For example, students may debate about what Robert Lewis Stevenson was really saying about human nature in The Strange Case of Dr. Jekyll and Mr. Hyde.

- Students can also explore drama by engaging in collaborative creative writing. The teacher can provide students with a list of influential playwrights throughout history such as Zora Neale Hurston, Thorton Wilder, William Shakespeare, Clare Luce Booth, Langston Hughes, Arthur Miller, Tennessee Williams, Gertrude Stein, Henrik Ibsen, and Sophocles. Each team may select a few plays to read and study and then generate a list of their critical dramatic elements. The team will then write their own play incorporating the dramatic elements they identified. Finally, each team will perform the play they wrote for the class. Class feedback and discussion should follow each performance.

- Another motivating group or whole-class activity requires student collaboration to create a historical newspaper. Each team will select one day in history, then investigate the events, authors, artists, and culture of that day. Based upon this information, they will create a newspaper that may includes such sections as World News, U.S. News, Editorials, Arts and Leisure, Sports, or any other section the team wishes to create. For example, a newspaper that represents February 15, 1929, will probably feature the previous day's St. Valentine's Day Massacre as a headline. Other front-page world and U.S. news may include reports on the recession of the automobile, steel, and rubber industries and Alexander Fleming's introduction of penicillin to cure bacterial infections. The Arts and Leisure section may feature stories about jazz artists Louis Armstrong or Bessie Smith and a movie review on The Taming of the Shrew starring Douglas Fairbanks and Mary Pickford. Book reviews of Eugene O'Neill's Strange Interlude or Nella Larson's Quicksand may also be included. This activity will provide students with an opportunity to work cooperatively as they develop a deeper understanding of historical context.

Discovering Your Voice

The previous independent and cooperative learning activities are primarily designed for students to build a solid foundation upon which to build their own originality while practicing their writing and communication skills. The "Discovering Your Voice" activities are designed to help your future great authors create their own original works. Specifically, students will examine the language, perspectives, and inspirations of their favorite authors as they work toward developing their own voices. An in-depth study of a piece of literature provides students with many launching points for examining their own perspectives, making personal connections, and producing their own inspired work. The following examples of Mary Shelley and Langston Hughes illustrate how to use a piece of literature to inspire written expression.

Mary Shelley

Since its publication in 1818, Mary Shelley's Frankenstein has been regarded as a novel of horror and science fiction. Many students are most familiar with the novel's protagonist: the nameless monster. Immortalized by 1930s Hollywood, the monster has become an icon for the dangers and hubris of unchecked scientific research. But, those who read the actual novel find that, while Frankenstein's monster does commit terrible acts, so does his creator. Both give birth to evil through their irresponsibility and their isolation.

Frankenstein's monster levels a terrible accusation at his maker: "How dare you thus sport with life? Do your duty towards me, and I will do mine towards you and the rest of mankind" (Shelley, 1818/1985, p. 145). "Sporting with life" serves as a focal point for the tension that exists between maker and monster. Frankenstein sports with life by creating and then abandoning his creature; the creature sports with life as he unsuccessfully attempts to participate in his creator's world. This tension opens up a wealth of writing opportunities within the gifted classroom. Students can explore Frankenstein from several vantage points often overlooked in the traditional English classroom. The following activities are designed to enhance gifted students' understanding of the novel and to encourage creative, critical writing.

After reading the novel, have students adopt the role of either Victor Frankenstein or the monster. Ask the students to justify their character's desire to "sport with life." Each student must write a defense, based on information supplied from the novel, of their character's actions either in creating life or in participating in it. Emphasize that these defense statements will serve as a starting point only and therefore do not need to be polished. Once the students are satisfied with their positions, ask them to break into pairs and debate each other. What kinds of reasons does Frankenstein give for creating life and then abandoning it? Why is the monster so determined to engage a society that does not accept him? As the students role-play, encourage them to jot down their opponent's rebuttal. Why can't the creator and his creation come to a meeting of the minds?

Once students have finished their debates, ask them to consider which character is more justified or more sympathetic. Which character is easiest for them to empathize with? Once they have chosen, have them take one more step and imagine a modern counterpart for their character. Current issues in the scientific community with cloning and harvesting embryos for stem cells will probably be the most obvious connection. But, students may think of other parallels such as teen pregnancy/parenthood, the responsibilities of the parents in light of school shootings, the welfare system, Big Brother government, the homeless and derelicts in urban centers, and even plastic surgeons. Encourage students to move beyond obvious connections and think of situations that impact them on a personal and emotional level.

Once the students have decided on a parallel issue, have them write their own short story in first-person narrative. Ask them to refer back to their defense positions as they create a character who either personifies the scientist/creator or the victim/monster. How does their character "sport with life" and what is the outcome? Does their story contain a moral or a warning? Or does is simply paint a vignette and allow the reader to decide?

Remind students that Mary Shelley does not have Victor Frankenstein tell his story directly to the reader. Rather, Robert

Walton, an explorer and seeker of unknown mysteries, tells the story through a series of letters to his sister. This stylistic device allows Walton to serve as a go-between for Frankenstein and the reader. Had Victor Frankenstein related his story directly, the reader would have questioned his objectivity and honesty. Although Shelley's novel contains a strong warning against irresponsible scientific pursuit, she lets the reader decide whether Frankenstein or his monster was justified in his actions. Have students consider adopting this same device by employing an outside narrator to convey their tale. What type of character is best suited to being objective, yet involved enough to offer accurate insight? Provide students with guidelines for story length as is appropriate for their weekly time in the gifted classroom. This activity should take approximately three to five class periods if students work on their stories at home and bring them to class for peer editing and revision. Consider having the students create covers for their stories and publish them using computer software.

Langston Hughes

As one of the first African American poets to support himself solely through writing, Langston Hughes remains a important voice in American literature. Hughes was a vital figure in the Harlem Renaissance in the 1920s and 1930s; early 20th-century African Americans hailed him as their Poet Laureate. His poetry was heavily influenced by the rhythms of Harlem jazz and blues. Hughes was a prolific writer, producing poetry, novels, short stories, plays, and newspaper pieces. One of the most outstanding qualities of his writing was his ability to stay true to his roots.

Poetry is meant to be read aloud; like music, it loses something of its power when left quiet on the page. Students can hear several of Hughes' poems read by the author at the Academy of American Poets' Web site (http://www.poets.org). The jazz and blues of 1920s Harlem influenced Hughes' poems, but his poetry, in turn, influenced the jazz of his day. In 1961, he wrote Ask Your Mama: 12 Moods for Jazz as a book of poems to be read to a jazz accompaniment. While the original sound recording is no longer available, The Langston Hughes Project provides excerpts from a multimedia show featuring the poems set to jazz (http://www. ronmccurdy.com). Students can listen and get a feel for the way Hughes' poetry sounds when read to a jazz tempo.

Langston Hughes published his first poem, "The Negro Speaks of Rivers," in 1921 at the age of 19. It remains one of his most famous pieces. Select a student to read "The Negro Speaks of Rivers" aloud. Discuss the natural rhythm and cadence used by the speaker as he or she reads. Does the poem provide its own "beat" for the reader to follow? Next, play a jazz selection while another student reads the same poem aloud. Does the addition of music affect the reading? In what ways?

Have students examine the structure and content of the poem. Hughes spoke from what he knew personally and historically about African Americans geographically. He used major rivers to emphasize the important cultural part Africans have played in civilization. Thus, Hughes paid tribute to the generations of African Americans who were dehumanized and marginalized through slavery and Jim Crow laws. Remind students that Hughes wrote this poem (as well as his other works) for himself. Have them read a selection from "The Negro Artist and the Racial Mountain" and reflect on Hughes' audience for this poem. For whom did he write it? Did he write it to inspire other African Americans? To jolt White Americans into rethinking segregation? Or did he write it for himself, to immortalize his own beliefs about the African American role in world history? These types of questions will generate discussion from which students can begin exploring where they fit in the scheme of civilization. Ask students to use Hughes' poem as a template for creating their own poetry. Play jazz in the background as they brainstorm and begin writing.

If students have difficulty making a cultural connection like Hughes', consider asking these questions: What is the student's ethnic heritage? Native Americans, Asians, and Hispanics have all played major roles the history of the United States. Caucasian students may find this cultural connection harder to make, but the Irish, the Scots, and the Germans played major roles in the westward expansion of the 19th century, as did those from the Scandinavian countries. Students can do informal research into their cultural roots; events such as the building of the transcontinental railroad and the California Gold Rush are rich with ethnic/cultural stories. Immigrant workers who migrated across the United States during the Great Depression made lasting impressions in the areas where they settled.

Once students have determined a topic they want to develop, have them begin writing their poetry, using "The Negro Speaks of Rivers" as a beginning template. Hughes was influenced by Harlem jazz; have students reflect on the music that influences and inspires them. Have them work on writing a poem that can be read to music they choose. Encourage them to find their voices and write to please themselves.

Conclusion

Mary Wollstonecraft Shelley and Langston Hughes were profoundly influenced by what they read, as were their writing styles. Research supports that good readers make good writers whose written expression is more sophisticated and syntactically mature (Stosky, 1983). Mary Shelley came from a family of writers: her mother wrote Vindication of the Rights of Women; her father was a novelist and political writer. She married the poet Percy Bysshe Shelley and was friends with Samuel Taylor Coleridge. Their works, as well as the works of scientists and classicists, shaped and influenced her writing. Langston Hughes found inspiration in the works of Paul Laurence Dunbar, Carl Sandburg, and Walt Whitman—poets who remained true to their poetic voices regardless of public response.

Had such classifications been available in their day, Langston Hughes and Mary Shelley would have been identified as creatively gifted students. Their intellect, voracious appetite for books, and constant desire to write down what they saw and felt and believed set them apart from other 19-year-olds both then and now. The gifted students in our schools have the same potential, and exposing them to the literary masters and giving them the opportunity to find their voices and express their beliefs and feelings is a powerful tool for learning.

References

Cixous, H. (1990). Difficult joys. In H. Wilcox, K. McWatters, A. Thompson, & L. R. Williams (Eds.), The body and the text: Helene Cixous, reading and teaching (pp. 5–30). New York: Harvester Wheatsheaf.

Corden, R. (2000). Reading-writing connections: The importance of interactive discourse. English in Education, 34, 35–44.

DeFord, D. E. (1981). Literacy: Reading, writing, and other essentials. Language Arts, 58, 652–658.

Fasko, D. (2000/2001). Education and creativity. Creative Research Journal, 13, 317–327.

Flower, L. (1990). The role of task representation in reading-to-write. In V. S. L. Flower, J. Ackerman, M. J. Kantz, K. McCormick, & W.C. Peck (Eds.), Reading-to-write: Exploring a cognitive and social process. New York: Oxford University Press.

Fraser, D. (2003). From the playful to the profound: What metaphors tell us about gifted children. Roeper Review, 25, 180–185.

Hollingworth, L. S. (1938). An enrichment curriculum for rapid learners at Public School 500, Speyer School. Teachers College Record, 39, 296–305.

Kauffman, J. C., & Gentile, C. A. (2002). The will, the wit, the judgement: The importance of an early start in productive and successful creative writing. High Ability Studies, 13, 115–124.

Kline, A. G. (2000). Fitting the school to the child: The mission of Leta Stetter Hollingworth, founder of gifted. Roeper Review, 23, 97–104.

Lee, I. (2000). Exploring reading-writing connections through a pedagogical focus on "coherence." Canadian Modern Language Review, 57, 352–56.

National Commission on Writing in America's Schools and Colleges. (2003, April). The neglected "R": The need for a writing revolution. Retrieved January 19, 2005, from http://www.writingcommission. org/prod_downloads/writingcom/ neglectedr.pdf

Renzulli, J. S., Smith, L. H., White, A. J., Callahan, C. M., Hartman, R. K., & Westberg, K. L. (2002). Scales for rating the behavioral characteristics of superior students (Rev ed.). Mansfield Center, CT: Creative Learning Press.

Shelley, M. (1985). Frankenstein. London: Penguin Books. (Original work published 1818)

Stotsky, S. (1983). Research on reading/writing relationships: A synthesis and suggested directions. Language Arts, 60, 636.

VanTassel-Baska, J. (1989). Appropriate curriculum for gifted learners. Educational Leadership, 46, 13–16.

VanTassel-Baska, J. (2003). Differenti-ating the language arts for high ability learners, K–8 (ERIC Digest ED 474 306). Retrieved January 19, 2005, from http://ericec.org/digests/ e640.html

Appendix A
Important Literaty Authors by Period and Culture

	Beginnings to 1st Century A.D.	2nd Century to 15th Century	16th Century (1500s)	17th Century (1600s)	18th Century (1700s)	19th Century (1800s)	20th Century (1900s)
Indian Subcontinent	Manu, Valmiki	Chandidas, Kabir	The Ghazal	Khan Khushal		Ghalib	Ghandi; Premchand
Chinese	I Ching, Confucius, Lao Tzu	Tao Yuanming, Xie Lingyun	Yangming Wang, Wu Chengen	Hong Shen	Yuan Mei, Cao Xueqin		Mao Tse-tung; Lin Yutang
Japanese	Manyoshu	Zeami	Kojiro Kanze	Matsuo Basho	Hakuin	Natsume Soseki	Mishima Yuko
Middle Eastern	Gilgamesh, Book of the Dead, The Bible	Talmud, Jami	Thousand and One Nights	Evliya Celebi			J. T. Tialrion, David Shar, Amos Oz
Greek	Homer, Aesop, Sophocles, Euripides	Anna Comnena, Ptolemy, Galen, Porphyry					C. P. Cavafy; George Sefens
Latin	Virgil, Ovid, Cicero	Anselm, St Aquinas, St Augustine	Erasmus, Thomas Moore, John Calvin	Johann Kepler, Baruch Spinoza	Carolus Linnaeus		Pope Pius X, XI, XII
Germanic		Nibelungenlied, Van Eschenbach, Von Strassburg	Martin Luther	Johann Gimmelshausen	Emmanuel Kant, Friedrich Von Schiller	Goethe, Brothers Grimm, Karl Marx, Heinrich Ibsen	Rainer Maria Rilke, Bertolt Brecht, Albert Schweitzer
French		Le Chanson de Roland, Jean Froissart, Philippe de Commynes	Robert Garnier, Marguerite de Navarre, Pierre de Ronsard	Descartes, Moliere, Pascal, Madame de la Fayette	Voltaire, Rousseau, Denis Diderot	Balzac, Victor Hugo, George Sand, Gustave Flaubert, Emile Zola	Marcel Proust, Jean Paul Sartre, Simone de Beauvoir, Albert Camus
Spanish, Portuguese		Juan Ruiz, Jorge Manrique, Gil Vicente Ferrera	Cervantes, Fernando de Rojas, Antonia Ferrera	Tirso de Molina, Luis de Gongora, Sister Juana Inez		Leopoldo Alas, Benito Perez Galdos	Gabriel Marquez, Carlos Fuentes
Italian		Dante Alighieri, Christine de Pizan	Machiavelli, Ludovico Ariosto	Tommaso Campa-nella, Galileo	Giacomo Casanova, Vittorio Alfieri	Giovanni Verga, Ugo Foscolo	Natalia Ginzburg, Primo Levi
Slavic						Pushkin, Tolstoy, Dostoyevsky, Chekhov	Pasternak, Bruno, Schultz, Gorky, Anna Akhmatova
English (British Isles)		Beowulf, Geoffrey Chaucer, Thomas Malory, William Dunbar	Sir Thomas Wyatt, Edmund Spencer, Christopher Marlow, Thomas Nashe	Francis Bacon, Shakespeare, John Donne, Thomas Hobbes, John Milton, John Locke	Johathan Swift, Mary Wollstonecraft, Adam Smith, Alexander Pope	William Blake, Coleridge, Jane Austin, Bronte Sisters, Mary Shelley, Dickens	Virginia Woolf, H. G. Wells, E. M. Forster, George Orwell, Dylan Thomas, Kipling
English (North America)				Anne Bradstreet, John Eliot, Cotton Mather, Samuel Danforth	Thomas Jefferson, Phyllis Wheatley, Thomas Paine, Benjamin Franklin, James Granger	Hawthorne, Poe, Twain, Melville, Emily Dickinson, Walt Whitman, Kate Chopin, Henry James, L. M. Alcott, Frederick Douglas	Maya Angelou, J. D. Salinger, Tennesse Williams, Steinbeck, Gertrude Stein, Sinclair Lewis, William Faulkner, F. Scott Fitzgerald

Appendix B
Examples of Literature Genres

Allegory	Adventure	Comedy	Chronicle	Epic	Fantasy
Religious Dante Alighieri, *The Divine Comedy* (1320); Faulkner, *A Fable* (1954); John Bunyan, *The Pilgrim's Progress* (1684) **Symbolic** Melville, *Moby Dick* (1851) **Philosophical** Kafka, *The Castle* (1926); Goethe, *Faust* (1808/1831) **Moral** Henry James, *The Turn of the Screw* (1898)	**Heroic** *The Epic of Gilgamesh* (2000 B.C.); *Hercules and His Twelve Labors* (unknown); Homer, *Odyssey* (6th century B.C.)	Shakespeare, *Comedy of Errors* (1592); Moliere, *Tartuffe* (1664) **Social** Jane Austin, *Emma* (1816) **Romantic** Aristophanes, *Lysistrata* (411 B.C.) **Comedy of manners** Oscar Wilde, *The Importance of Being Earnest* (1895); Moliere, *The Misanthrope* (1666); Jane Austin, *Pride and Prejudice* (1813)	**Historical** Willa Cather, *Death Comes for the Archbishop* (1927); Shakespeare, *Henry the Fourth* (1597) **Regional** John Steinbeck, *East of Eden* (1952); Willa Cather, *My Antonia* (1918) **Social Chronicle** Pearl S. Buck, *The Good Earth*; (1931) Victor Hugo, *Les Misérables* (1862) **Philosophical** Thomas Mann, *The Magic Mountain* (1924)	**Heroic** *Beowulf* (1000); Virgil, *Aeneid* (70-19 B.C.); Homer, *Iliad* (6th century B.C.); *Mahabharata* (5th century); *The Nibelungenlied* (1200) **Religious** Valmiki, *Ramayana* (350 B.C.)	Lewis Carroll, *Alice's Adventures in Wonderland* (1865); Anatole France, *Penguin Island* (1908); Robert Lewis Stevenson, *The Strange Case of Dr. Jekyll and Mr. Hyde* (1886); H. G. Wells, *The Time Machine* (1895); Kafka, *The Trial* (1925); Samuel T. Coleridge, *The Rime of the Ancient Mariner* (1798)

Naturalism	Realism	Romance	Satire	Social Criticism	Tragedy
Honore de Balzac, *Eugénie Grandet* (1833); *Pere Goriot* (1835); Emile Zola, *Germinal* (1865); Strindberg, *Miss Julie* (1888); Arnold Bennett, *The Old Wives' Tale* (1908)	**Psychological** William Faulkner, *As I Lay Dying* (1930); Virginia Woolf, *Mrs. Dalloway* (1925); Henry James, *The Portrait of a Lady* (1881); Dostoevsky, *Crime and Punishment* (1886); George Eliot, *Middlemarch* (1872) **Philosophical** Jean-Paul Sartre, *Nausea* (1938); Thomas Hardy, *Tess of D'Urbervilles* (1891) **Impressionistic** Stephen Crane, *Red Badge of Courage* (1895); Dostoevsky, *The Brothers Karamazov* (1880)	**Adventure** Mark Twain, *The Adventures of Tom Sawyer* (1876); Rudyard Kipling, *Kim* (1901); Daniel Defoe, *Robinson Crusoe* (1719) **Psychological** Charlotte Bronte, *Jane Eyre* (1847); Nathaniel Hawthorne, *The Scarlet Letter* (1850) **Chivalric** Chaucer, *Canterbury Tales* (1390) **Historical** Victor Hugo, *The Hunchback of Notre Dame* (1831); James Feminore Cooper, *Last of the Mohicans* (1826) **Gothic** Edgar Allan Poe, *The Fall of the House of Usher* (1839); Mary Shelley, *Frankenstein* (1818)	**Social** Johnathan Swift, *Gulliver's Travels* (1726); Nikolai Gogol, *Dead Souls* (1855); Sinclair Lewis, *Babbitt* (1922); Anthony Trollope, *Barchester Towers* (1857); Aristophanes, *The Birds* (414 B.C.); Voltaire, *Candide* (1759) **Political** George Orwell, *Nineteen Eighty Four* (1949) **Humorous** Mark Twain, *Huckleberry Finn* (1884)	E. M. Forster, *A Passage to India* (1924); Nikolai Gogol, *The Overcoat* (1842); Leo Tolstoy, *Anna Karenina* (1877); Henrik Ibsen, *A Doll's House* (1879); John Steinbeck, *Grapes of Wrath* (1939); F. Scott Fitzgerald, *The Great Gatsby* (1925)	**Symbolic** Herman Melville, *Billy Budd* (1924) **Classical** Sophocles, *Antigone* (441 B.C.); Euripides, *The Bacchae* (405 B.C.); *Medea* (431 B.C.); Jean Racine, *Phaedra* (1677); Aeschylus, *Prometheus Bound* (5th century) **Romantic** Shakespeare, *Julius Caesar* (1601); *Romeo and Juliet* (1595); Christopher Marlowe, *Doctor Faustus* (1588); Thomas Hardy, *The Return of the Native* (1878); Strassburg, *Tristan and Isolde* (1210) **Domestic** Edith Wharton, *Ethan Fromme* (1911)

Appendix C
Examples of Literary Movements
in the 19th and 20th Centuries

Movement	Time Period	Description	Authors
Aestheticism	1800s France England	"art for art's sake," not combined with political or moral teaching	Oscar Wilde, Charles Baudelaire, Marcel Proust
Beat Movement	1950s–1960s U.S.	rejection of established social and literary values, stream of consciousness writing, free verse influenced by jazz	Jack Kerouac, Allen Ginsberg, Lawrence Ferlinghetti
Black Aesthetic Movement	1960s–1970s U.S.	paralleled by civil rights movement, literature meaningful to the Black population	Haki R. Madhubuti, Sonia Sanchez
Celtic Renaissance	End of 1800s Ireland	romantic vision of Celtic myth and legend, dreamy, unreal world, reaction against the reality of contemporary problems	William Butler Yeats
Dadaism	Began in 1916 Europe	protest movement, outrage at the destruction of WWI, revolting against social convention, marked by calculated madness and flamboyant nonsense, freedom of expression	Andre Breton, Louis Aragon, Philippe, Paul Eluard
Existentialism	20th Century Europe	concerned with the nature and perception of human existence, anguish as a universal element of life, individuals must bear responsibility for actions	Franz Kafka, Fyodor Dostoyevsky, Simone de Beauvoir, Albert Camus
Expressionism	Early 1900s Europe	unconventional, highly subjective writing that distorts reality in some way	Eugene O'Neill, Ernst Stadler, James Joyce
Futurism	1908–1920 France, Italy, Russia	attempts to achieve total freedom of expression through bizarre imagery and deformed or newly invented words	Wyndham Lewis, Guillaume Apollinaire, Vladimir Mayakovsky
Harlem Renaissance	1920s U.S.	Black authors and artists received their first widespread recognition and serious critical appraisal	Langston Hughes, Zora Neale Hurston
Imagism	1908–1917 England, U.S.	used precise, clearly presented images; used common, everyday speech, aimed for concise, concrete imagery	Ezra Pound, Amy Lowell
Irish Literary Renaissance	Late 1800s, Early 1900s	attempted to reduce the influence of British Culture in Ireland, and create an Irish national literature	George Moore, Sean O'Casey
Modernism	Early 1900s U.S., Europe	rejection of the 19th-century literary conventions, opposition to conventional morality, taste, traditions, and economic values	D. H. Lawrence, Ernest Hemingway, Tennessee Williams
Naturalism	Late 1800s, Early 1900s Europe, U.S.	examines human life with the objectivity of scientific inquiry, focused on degradation: poverty, alcoholism, insanity, and disease	Thomas Hardy, Stephen Crane, Theodore Dreiser
Parnassianism	Mid-1800s France	adherence to well-defined artistic forms as a reaction against the often chaotic expression of the Romantics	Albert Glatigny, Francois Coppee
Post-Aesthetic	After 1970s U.S.	reaction to Black Aesthetic movement, portrayed African Americans looking inward for answers	Alice Walker, Toni Morrison, John Edgar Wideman,
Postmodernism	1960s forward	characterized by experimentation and application of the fundamentals of modernism, existentialism, alienation	Margaret Drabble, John Fowles, Gabriel Marquez
Realism	1900s Europe	reaction to romanticism, portrayal of familiar characters and settings in a realistic manner, using an objective narrative viewpoint	Honore de Balzac, Gustave Flaubert, George Eliot
Romanticism	Late 1800s to Early 1900s Europe	emotional and imaginative expression rather than rational analysis, devoted to individualistic expression, self-analysis, or a pursuit of higher knowledge	Jean-Jacque Rousseau, William Wordsworth, Lord Byron
Russian Realism	1894–1910 Russia	stressed aestheticism over didactic intent, saw selves as mediators of the supernatural and the mundane	Aleksandr Blok, Fyodor Sologub, Nikolay Gumilyov
Surrealism	1920s France	expressed unconscious thoughts and feelings, proposed to unify the contrary levels of dream and reality	Paul Eluard, Pierre Reverdy, Louis Aragon
Symbolism	1800s France, Ireland, England, U.S.	aimed to evoke an order of being beyond the material world, expressed the highly complex feelings that grew out of everyday contact with the world	Charles Baudelaire, Arthur Rimbaud, T. S. Eliot

chapter 10

Alternate Doorways

teaching writing to children with varied gifts

by **Sharon Black**

four-year-old Susan, enrolled in her first class in creative dance, could not seem to get past the problem of the pointed toe. Alternatively she lifted her toe toward the ceiling or curled it under, but she couldn't seem to achieve the graceful point that her teacher demonstrated. Susan wasn't a slow child; in fact, she had started reading at age 3, and she could pick out any tune she heard on the piano. But, her verbal and musical gifts did not seem to have much effect on her physical skills. She'd recently failed the "Beginner 1" swimming class, and now her dance teacher was sure that either she was hopelessly dense or she just wasn't trying.

"Reach—stretch," her older sister offered. From that cue, her mother had an idea: "Susie, pretend there's a jelly bean on the floor—right here—and your toe is sticky on the very tip. If you poke your toe up in the air, the jelly bean will roll back off your ankle, and you'll lose it. If you squeeze your toe under, the jelly bean will get sweaty and won't taste good. Just reach out and stick that jelly bean with the end of your toe."

Intrigued with the mental picture of the jelly bean, Susan reached and slightly twisted her toe into a pointed position. She never had trouble with the pointed toe again. She simply needed a mental picture and a way of reasoning verbally through what she was supposed to do.

Susan accessed learning through pictorial symbols and words rather than through seeing a body position and feeling it in her muscles as her dance teacher did. Neither the student nor the teacher lacked ability or sense; they just approached the task from different directions.

As Guild (1997) put it, "The bottom line is that learning is a complex process and students learn in various ways" (p. 31), a concept that Gardner (1997b) expanded: "Just as we look different from one another and have different kinds of personalities, we also have different kinds of minds" (p. 9). Because children think, reason, learn, and create in different ways, teachers need to present opportunities for children to both develop their gifts and strengthen their weaker areas.

Gardner (1983, 1997a) has referred to these varied opportunities as doorways through which children arrive at learning. This chapter will look at both the need for providing a variety of doorways and some of the specific doorways through which children may enter the learning experience. Writing, a skill that is often taught through only one doorway, but can be taught through many, will be treated in detail as a sample learning area.

Closed Doors, Heavy Doors

Susan was not unique or even unusual in the difficulty she experienced in learning skills (swimming, pointing her toe) that were introduced to her through methods by which her mind did not automatically process information.

In contrast, Gallas (1994) described a child with different gifts. Brian had been labeled ADHD because of his "constant motion and distractibility," but his teacher noted how he observed with uncharacteristic patience the transition of meal worm to pupa and imitated those movements with great accuracy: "Brian had the ability to translate his ideas into a kinetic modality. . . . Brian's strengths [include] how carefully he observes and analyzes every detail of the world around him, and how creatively he solves challenging problems" (p. 136).

Similarly, Voss (1996) described a gifted 10-year-old boy who could repair a broken electric train, but struggled behind grade level with reading. Voss' conclusion should be the goal of any parent or teacher: "I had to find *his* way of making meaning, rather than expect him to conform to mine" (p. 8).

Until teachers and parents learn to find the ways that their varying students *make meaning*, many children will find doors to some learning experiences closed—difficult and sometimes impossible to open. Many students who struggle with such doors are labeled "lazy" or "stubborn," when the actual problem is in a "cognitive mismatch" (Tucker, 1995, p. 27) between how they learn and how the learning experience is structured. Traditionally, education in schools has been primarily centered in language, logic, and mathematics (Gardner, 1983, 1991, 1993, 1997a), and children not strong in these areas receive an unfortunate message:

> Their natural way of understanding the world is not an important and valid way . . . part of the process of being educated is to exclude and isolate their most powerful means of making the world sensible and to adopt a more linear language style in which logic prevails. (Gallas, 1994, p. 116)

The fact that language is not a child's most natural way of making sense of the world does not mean the child lacks talent or potential. Gardner (1993) quoted Albert Einstein:

> The words of the language, as they are written or spoken, do not seem to play a role at all in my mechanism of thought. The psychical entities which seem to serve as elements in thought are certain signs and more or less clear images which can be "voluntarily" reproduced and combined. . . . Conventional words or other signs have to be sought for laboriously only in a secondary stage. (p. 105)

As McCarthy (1997) expressed it, "Learners speak in words, signs, symbols, movement, and through music" (p. 132).

Alternate Doors

Susan, the child who had difficulty learning to point her toe because kinesthetic activity was not her primary way of making sense of the world, eventually became a competent dancer and a strong choreographer. As she grew older and dance became a means by which she interpreted music, her natural gifts for music and for symbol systems were an integral part of her dance experience. Kinesthetic competence eventually developed through use and practice.

Possibly more common is the contrasting experience described by Lee (1994), a college instructor, in which Janet, a gifted and accomplished dancer, was self-conscious over the inadequacy of her words in expressing her ideas to her classmates, many of whom had strengths in verbal communication. As Lee stated, "I didn't want to know how 'smart' Janet was according to some predetermined standard; I wanted to know *how Janet was smart*" (p. 82; see also Hatch, 1997, p. 26). The class had been exploring consultation and collaboration as communication styles, and Lee encouraged Janet to portray her feelings and interpretations through dance. The result was a memorable experience in which Janet—with a half-mask, a pair of scissors, and the highly developed capacity of her body to portray feelings that eluded words—involved her classmates in aspects and emotions concerning consultation and collaboration that they had not anticipated, but were able to comprehend and share.

The experience was pivotal for both Janet and her classmates; all of them had a new standard, a new way of viewing Janet's competence. An alternate doorway had been offered to explore consultation and collaboration. As concepts explored through alternate means are verbalized within a group, verbal skills are strengthened along with thinking capabilities. When restricted to only one form of instruction and response, some students are denied the education they need (Gage, 1995, p. 53), as surely as a student in a wheelchair may be denied education if the only door to the school is at the top of a flight of stairs and no help is provided for the child to access it.

New Doorways

The house of learning has—or should have—many doors and many corridors. Merrefield (1997) suggested that, rather than identifying failings and weaknesses of students, teachers should "celebrate and capitalize on alternative forms of smartness . . . [in] a positive and respectful way" (p. 61). Thus, a teacher who is aware of and concerned for the varied minds of his or her students will attempt to provide enough variation within the shared learning experience for each to become involved (Gallas, 1994). An observant dance teacher might notice that little Susan's hand was the first to be raised when she asked the children to put their feelings about a piece of music into words. Appreciating Susan's verbal and musical gifts, she might approach Susan's unpointed toe with a verbal explanation, rather than a kinesthetic demonstration. In contrast, Campbell, Campbell, and Dickinson (1996) described a teacher who noticed the unusual physical grace of a child who had been labeled as slow and backward and encouraged her to create a "movement alphabet." By dancing her spelling words, the child was able to use her strong kinesthetic gifts to learn linguistic skills that had been difficult for her.

Complex, detailed diagnosis is not necessary, and a teacher need not put a label on each student (McCarthy, 1997). Experienced elementary teacher Karen Gallas (1994) advised that the teacher must simply "listen to the children." She explained, "They will show you what they know and how they learn best" (p. 132).

Does listening to each child mean that the teacher must provide a separate and unique curriculum for each child? Doing so would, of course, be impossible. It would be undesirable, as well. But, if students are allowed to choose comfortable doorways to enter some areas of their learning experience, they will be more willing to venture past additional doors as their experience expands. And, as McCarthy (1997) explained, "The more voices students master, the more learning they will do" (p. 132).

Alternate Doorways to the Writing Experience

Writing, a linguistic skill, is traditionally taught through linguistic experiences. Gallas (1994) illustrated the use of an alternate doorway when she told of Juan, a child who had recently moved to the United States from Venezuela. He spoke little English, but he drew fluently and eloquently.

> His visual representations became a catalogue of science information and science questions, and that information began to provide material for his involvement in reading and writing and learning a new language. As Juan drew, we built a reading and speaking vocabulary from his pictures, and that vocabulary, together with his interest in representing science, also became the subject matter of his writing. (p. 132)

For Juan, drawing—a visual representation—was an entry point that used his natural strengths in visual and kinesthetic areas to develop areas of less strength.

Juan is not unique or even unusual. Writing skill depends heavily on linguistic talents to generate words and sentences that express ideas, and it also depends on linear abilities to organize those ideas into structures that can be easily received and interpreted by readers. Traditionally, writing has been difficult or impossible for children like Juan who are particularly deficient in these areas, though they may be gifted in others. However, since writing expresses ideas, experience, and knowledge, it is a skill area that can be approached through a variety of ideas, experiences, and forms of knowledge. Thus, students can enter writing competence by a variety of doorways.

Multisensory Doorways

Almost all children are responsive to sensory input; however, the degree of awareness and differentiation involved with sensory experience will vary, with some children favoring one sense, some favoring another. Multisensory experiences are easy to share, and they can naturally generate language (and enthusiasm). Shared sensory activities and experiences prior to a writing session provide a number of entry points to the practice and development of writing skills.

A simple, yet motivating multisensory experience for young children is to brainstorm words that describe an object. A piece of gummi candy—especially a gummi worm—immediately engages almost all of the senses because of the candy's translucent, variegated colors; its slightly slimy-smooth surface with distinct ridges; its fruity smell; and its tart-sweet flavor. Auditory involvement can be produced by manipulating it on or slapping it against surfaces. As words are suggested to represent the sensory impressions, students use their sense-dominant abilities to access and share language. If the teacher will make brief and humorous remarks and invite student comment on the varied and interesting words, group cohesion is increased and momentum is generated for finding additional words. Keeping the tone of the experience light and humorous will naturally generate word play, which is an effective way to promote linguistic development. When the teacher writes the words on the chalkboard or on chart paper, an informal reading lesson is also involved, and a word bank is provided for writing activities.

The shared sensory experience can be extended to writing projects as students write descriptions of the object or make up stories or poems about it using some of the words from the brainstormed list. Giving the children a choice of these genres allows still more opportunities to use alternative ways to think and create. Straightforward description emphasizes visual acuity and linear thought; a narrative places more value on the expressive and imaginative uses of language and detail; and a poem brings out musical properties of language more vividly than most forms of prose. Thus, the children enter the experience with varied senses and work some of their more abstract and complex abilities once they get inside.

As children become older, shared sensory experiences become more complex. Thomas Haggitt (1967), a junior high school English teacher, suggested taking children outside and having them experience the weather with all of their senses. Wind, rain, fog, or snow can produce a wide range of sensory impressions, as well as situational details, that the children can describe. Haggitt had 7-year-olds begin with lists of everything they saw, heard, touched, smelled, and tasted; he taught older children to focus on how the details blend into more unified impressions. Even the younger children soon learned to think figuratively (e.g., the wind as an angry man or a cruel beast).

Shared experiences can be as simple as a walk around the school playground or a nearby park, and they can be as complex as a field trip to a farm, a bakery, or a fire station. Students can take detailed multisensory field notes on the growth and habits of classroom pets, ranging from rabbits to newts. Most children get excited over a cooking experience; teachers commonly cook with the group to make practical application of math or reading skills or to illustrate science concepts—why not brainstorm words to describe how things look, feel, sound, smell, and especially taste at various stages of the process? Any of these experiences can be extended into a variety of writing genres, including a personal journal, an expository report, or a set of instructions. One class went from describing their class newts to writing fiction stories narrating the adventures of "Wayne and Fig."

Doors and Corridors of Performance

Language skills can develop as by-products of drama, dance, music, and art because words are blended into experiences that may come more naturally to some of the children than the words themselves. Teachers at an elementary school in Utah experimented with involving children in drama and art as prewriting activities; they found that these children's writing was at least as skilled and effective as the writing of children who had participated in extensive discussions and that motivation and interest were increased (B. Moore, personal communication, October, 1991).

Children with strong interpersonal abilities can often explore ideas more naturally through role-play than through pencil play, as they interact with others in realistic circumstances to solve real-life problems (e.g., a conversation between two people who have witnessed an act of dishonesty and need to decide whether they should take action). Such a role-play might be the beginning of a script for a play written collaboratively by several classmates or a variety of creative stories, newspaper articles, personal letters, or personal essays—any of which would translate the thinking generated by the role-play performance into a written product. Again, giving the students a choice of products would allow them to use areas of personal strength as settings for developing linguistic and organizational skills.

Storytelling is a form of performance that has much intrinsic appeal for children. It goes a step beyond story reading in providing varied doorways, as the impact depends on the connection between the face, voice, and words of the teller and the attention and imagination of the listener. Many seasoned storytellers have described the experience as an act of cocreation between the teller and the listeners (Baker & Greene, 1987; Nelson, 1989). They explain that the listeners should receive the story as a series of moving pictures (Barton, 1986; Breneman & Breneman, 1983); some advise that the teller should prepare the story as a series of pictures to describe, rather than as a sequence of words to reproduce (Cooter, 1991).

If the teacher prepares a story carefully in order to convey mental pictures, the children can receive and cocreate it using varied strengths and talents as entry points into the language experience. Then, as children share their own stories, the involvement of multiple talents becomes a more intensely creative experience. The emphasis on word pictures and, thus, on picture words develops linguistic abilities in terms of visual talents. Kinesthetic abilities are also involved as students learn to describe action in vivid and specific ways. Putting the pictures together in clear and logical sequences uses logical and mathematical abilities, although students will probably not be aware of it. Of course, those with musical talents have an opportunity to share the musical properties of language. As experienced storyteller Bob Barton (1986) has remarked, "The sound and rhythm of the words are often all part of the meaning" (p. 45).

In addition, some students have strong interpersonal abilities that enable them to relate well to the audience and anticipate the audience's response to aspects of their performance; these individuals have an opportunity to utilize and polish their natural talents in tandem with the verbal skills they may need to strengthen. If singing, chanting, drums, dancing, pantomime, or puppetry can be added to the storytelling experience, still more talents are included in the linguistic-logical-visual-kinesthetic-musical-interpersonal blend. Once the students have entered by varying doorways and traveled through the multifaceted corridor of the storytelling activity, the stories can be written and published as a class collection to which everyone has contributed.

Conclusion

Linda Campbell (1997), experienced in both elementary and secondary teaching, has commented:

> A school is responsible for helping all students discover and develop their talents or strengths. In doing this, the school not only awakens children's joy in learning but also fuels the persistence and effort necessary for mastering skills and information and for being inventive. (p. 14)

Without the opportunity to access learning through their own ways of thinking and knowing, many students have no motivation to put forth this persistence and effort. Many come to view their diversity as inferiority, and they make little effort because they anticipate little success.

Four-year-old Susan could not understand how some of her classmates could see a dance step performed and simply move their bodies in the same pattern without thinking through or verbalizing what that pattern was. Some of these classmates could not understand how Susan could see pictures in her mind when the teacher played music or could find tunes on a piano with no written notes. Students are unique in their strengths and learning abilities, and if they are allowed to learn, think, and contribute through their individual gifts—celebrating, rather than hiding, their diversity—significant learning and development will occur.

References

Baker, A., & Greene, E. (1987). *Storytelling: Art and technique* (2nd ed.). London: Bowker.

Barton, B. (1986). *Tell me another: Storytelling and reading aloud at home, at school, and in the community.* Portsmouth, NH: Heinemann.

Breneman, L. N., & Breneman, B. (1983). *Once upon a time: A storytelling handbook.* Chicago: Nelson Hall.

Campbell, L. (1997). Variations on a theme: How teachers interpret MI theory. *Educational Leadership, 55*(1), 14–21.

Campbell, L., Campbell, B., & Dickinson, D. (1996). *Teaching & learning through multiple intelligences*. Needham Heights, MA: Allyn and Bacon.

Cooter, R. B. (1991). Storytelling in the language arts classroom. *Reading Research and Instruction, 30*(2), 71–76.

Gage, R. (1995). Excuse me, you're cramping my style: Kinesthetics for the classroom. *English Journal, 84*(8), 52–55.

Gallas, K. (1994). *The languages of learning*. New York: Teachers College, Columbia University

Gardner, H. (1983). *Frames of mind: The theory of multiple intelligences*. New York: BasicBooks.

Gardner, H. (1991). *The unschooled mind*. New York: BasicBooks.

Gardner, H. (1993). *Creating minds: An anatomy of creativity seen through the lives of Freud, Einstein, Picasso, Eliot, Graham, and Ghandi*. New York: BasicBooks.

Gardner, H. (1997a). *Beyond multiple intelligences*. General session at the annual meeting of the Association for Supervision and Curriculum Development, Baltimore, MD.

Gardner, H. (1997b). The first seven . . . and the eighth. *Educational Leadership, 55*(1), 8–13.

Guild, P. B. (1997). Where do the learning theories overlap? *Educational Leadership, 55*(1), 30–31.

Haggitt, T. W. (1967). *Working with language*. Oxford, England: Blackwell.

Hatch, T. (1997). Getting specific about multiple intelligences. *Educational Leadership, 54*(6), 26–29.

Lee, P. A. (1994). To dance one's understanding. *Educational Leadership, 51*(5), 81–83.

McCarthy, B. (1997). A tale of four learners: 4MAT's learning styles. *Educational Leadership, 54*(6), 46–51.

Merrefield, G. E (1997). Three billy goats and Gardner. *Educational Leadership, 55*(1), 58–61.

Nelson, O. (1989). Storytelling: Language experience for meaning making. *The Reading Teacher, 42*, 386–390.

Tucker, B. (1995). Minds of their own: Visualizers compose. *English Journal, 84*(8), 27–30.

Voss, M. M. (1996). *Hidden literacies*. Portsmouth, NH: Heinemann.

chapter 11

A Writers' Workshop for Highly Verbal Gifted Students

by **Cecile P. Frey**

n 1989, the Carnegie Corporation of New York published *Turning Points: Preparing American Youth for the 21st Century*, one of the first documents to give credibility and visibility to middle-level education. The report recommended, among other "turning points," that middle schools "ensure success for all students." Although this recommendation can be taken as a warning not to ignore "high-risk" or special-education students, gifted students also fit into this category. As Plucker and McIntire (1996) pointed out, "Although researchers have found that students of all ability levels are bored in school, high-potential students are especially affected by a lack of challenge in the classroom" (p. 7). The more highly gifted the student, the more likely he or she is to be bored.

The ideas incorporated into the Carnegie report were expanded by later groups, most notably by the National Middle School Association (NMSA) in *This We Believe: Developmentally Responsive Middle Schools* (1995): "Developmentally responsive middle level schools provide curriculum that is challenging, integrative, and exploratory; varied teaching and learning approaches; assessment and evaluation that promote learning; flexible organizational structures; and comprehensive guidance and support services" (p. 11). Emphasis is placed on educators who "make sound pedagogical decisions based on the needs, interests, and special abilities of their students. They are sensitive to individual differences and respond positively to the natural diversity present in middle level classrooms" (p. 13). There is also the stated belief that "successful middle level schools are grounded in understanding that young adolescents are capable of far more than adults often assume" (p. 15). Promoting high achievement "requires adults to start where students are, understanding their individual needs, interests, and learning styles, then fashion a substantive curriculum and pace of learning to meet individual levels of understanding" (p. 16).

However, most middle school classes are heterogeneously grouped and practice inclusion (including students with learning and behavioral challenges), making it difficult for classroom teachers to address the needs of all the students in the class. Too often, gifted students must fend for themselves in these classes, reading the "class novel" at the same pace as everyone else and "demonstrating knowledge and understanding" by completing the same assignments and projects.

The goals for identified gifted students in middle schools are many. Educators and parents want them to learn to value intellectual achievement and develop scholarly behaviors and habits of mind. There is a strong recognition that gifted students at all levels, especially in middle school, need emphasis placed on depth and complexity of materials. Further, they also need to balance cognitive and psychosocial needs, understanding who they are and what they want for themselves, both in the long run and the short run. Many need to "experience personal connectedness to the curriculum and instruction in which they are participants" (Smith, 1999, p. 13). The fear of parents and caring educators is that, if gifted students turn off to school during the middle years, they cannot be rescued in high school when the work becomes more difficult and they lack the work ethic all students must have in order to be successful in their classes.

How and Why "Writers' Workshop" Began

Several years ago, a middle school principal in our district asked for help with six highly verbal gifted students whose needs could not be met in the regular eighth-grade program. Each of the four boys and two girls had a verbal intelligence score above 145 on the WISC-III. Since middle school language arts classes are heterogeneously grouped, even enrichment and "special work" did not seem enough for these students, all of whom were voracious readers and outstanding writers.

Because I had begun my teaching career as a high school English teacher, this challenge seemed like an opportunity to see how far these students could be stretched, so I agreed to meet with them 1 hour a week for the remainder of the school year. At the time, I did not know any of the students personally; I knew only that their experienced English teachers had recommended that they be included in the group and that the students were "chomping at the bit" to take on challenging work. I spoke with their English teachers in advance regarding meeting times. The teachers, parents, and administrators agreed that the group could meet one period per week. Since the school was on a rotating schedule, this meant they would miss each regular class only once every 5 weeks. The students agreed to make up work they missed.

At our first meeting, we mutually agreed on a set of informal rules, which could be modified as needed. I wanted the class to be student-driven and saw myself as a mentor and a facilitator, rather than a teacher in the traditional sense of the word. At the same time, I did not want this class to turn into a "he said, she said" gossip mill, where the students would view it as an opportunity to get out of class. We drafted the following goals together:

1. Regular attendance, with readings that we had agreed to complete before the next meeting.
2. Regular, appropriate participation.
3. Written assignments we agreed to complete.
4. Contribution of at least one original work (poem, essay, short story) to be used for class discussion. Each week, one student planned to share his or her work for the workshop

portion of the class. (Not once did any student fail to arrive with a draft of a poem, short story, or essay.)

5. Maintenance of a folder or notebook with materials we were using so that we could refer to past readings as needed.

The mission statement of the group reflected these goals: "The class will *not* be graded; it will just be a place where we can all talk about our common interests in writing and writers."

The Readings

I offered to choose the first readings and asked the students to read "Harrison Bergeron" from *Welcome to the Monkey House* (Vonnegut, 1968) for the following week. My goal was for them not only to read the story, but also to analyze it in terms of plot, character, setting, and theme. As potential writers, I felt they needed to understand the *structure* of successful short stories so that they might adapt some of the techniques to their own writing. I wanted to make sure they knew *how* to read in the deepest sense of the word, rather than merely being able to repeat what the story said and who said what to whom. I felt they were also ready to learn to relate the context (e.g., social and political climate) to the story. Because I did not know how able they were to think critically and analytically, I prepared the following questions for discussion in case the conversation lagged:

1. Why did the story cause a stir? What was life like in the U.S. in 1961? In the 1950s?
2. What is Vonnegut's theme? What techniques did he use to make clear what the story represented?
3. Is the theme of this story still applicable today? Why or why not?
4. Are the people in the story characters or caricatures? How do you know?
5. What would you have done differently in the story to get the point across more clearly?

Although I had been a teacher of gifted students for more than 25 years, I was astonished by the students' understanding and analysis. Many adolescents read superficially, usually for the plot, but do not (or cannot) probe the material in any depth. To avoid that kind of reading, we discussed how people read and the importance of reflecting on difficult pieces instead of merely skimming. I also pointed out that skimming was fine for certain kinds of reading, but not for literature as meaty as what we were discussing. These students were also able to bring their independent reading into the discussion, suggesting books and short stories on similar themes. In fact, an offshoot of the group was that they became a sort of lending library, sharing with each other books they were enjoying on their own. They also evolved into an informal book club, comparing what they were reading on their own at the beginning and end of class and on e-mail. From the first session, I could see that these students were far more capable than I thought they would be. Their seriousness of purpose negated my stereotypical vision of giggly eighth-grade girls and itchy boys.

The following week they read "The Lottery" by Shirley Jackson (1992), again at my recommendation. We discussed the theme carefully with much emphasis on the roles of leaders and followers. Why did the town continue the stoning year after year? What other stories did this remind you of (e.g., "The Emperor's New Clothes")? What superstitions exist that you follow today and are unwilling to give up even though they may seem silly? Again, the discussion was deep and meaningful, and the students seemed grateful to be able to have a serious discussion with other students who had similar interests and abilities.

The selection of "The Lottery" was the last choice that was totally mine. Since we had been reading short stories, one of the girls suggested that we read some O. Henry (1991), one of her favorite writers. We read "The Green Door" and "The Yellow Dog," as most of them had already read "Gift of the Magi" in their regular classes. This gave us an opportunity to examine the similarities in O. Henry's stories. We also talked about prolific authors (they were all reading Stephen King on their own at the time) and how common threads and differences keep the reader returning to an author even though she or he knows the format of the book in advance. As a long-time reader of mysteries, I was able to tell them why mystery novels are so appealing to me and what authors I read again and again. We seriously discussed the question, "What makes you keep coming back to an author or a series?"

The final short story we read was "The Pit and the Pendulum" by Edgar Allan Poe (1999). One of the students had just gone on a Poe tear, reading through many of his stories at home. We talked about Poe's writing, his introduction of the mystery genre in the U.S., and his own sad life. Afterwards, several of us went home and read some of Poe's other stories, as well as some of his poetry.

Since many of the students were already writing poetry on their own, I asked whether they'd like to read some published poems. When they readily agreed, I gathered a packet of poems I love along with explanations of the differences between poetry and prose and some of the basic elements found in poems (see Norton & Gretton, 1972, pp. 101–198). Again, they surprised me by bringing in poems they particularly liked. These included such unlikely authors as Ted Berrigan, Sylvia Plath, and John Ashbery. We read some traditional, metered poetry (e.g., some of Shakespeare's sonnets) and moved on to "Richard Cory" by Edward Arlington Robinson (1973); "This is Just to Say," by William Carlos Williams (1978); "Death of the Hired Man" by Robert Frost (1979); and "How Everything Happens (Based on a Study of the Wave)" by May Swenson (1978). We spent a good deal of time discussing the topic of what makes a poem, since some of the poems seemed disjointed and elliptical. By the end of the poetry sessions, students could demonstrate a better feel for poetry, especially modern poetry, and they were beginning to experiment with new styles of poetry writing, as well.

I also shared copies of stories, poems, and art that had won Scholastic Writing Awards, which are published each May in *Literary Cavalcade*. The students chose what they liked and didn't like, and we used both groups for careful analysis. We asked: "Why do you think the judges selected this? How would you change it to make it more effective?" This added dimension, where students could read the work of others not much older than they, gave them an additional framework for analyzing their own writing and the materials they were reading.

After poetry, one of the students, a professional actor, asked whether we could read some plays. I was pleased that students wanted to explore another genre and suggested they start with

Our Town by Thornton Wilder (1957). They appreciated the characters, but found the play as a whole dated and childish. Since the actor had appeared in *A Doll's House*, he suggested we read Ibsen (1969). We started with *A Doll's House*, discussing Nora's character in detail, both in light of the age in which she lived and in terms of her motivation, and then moved to *Ghosts*, which was less well known to them and, in some ways, more disturbing. They handled it with aplomb, however, and found both plays interesting, but dated.

Since they wanted to read something more modern, we read *An American Dream* and *The Zoo Story* by Edward Albee (1961). Although the writing was more elliptical and the characters more dense and disturbed, the students were able to grasp the essence of both plays and state what they liked or didn't like about the characters and themes in specific terms. We decided on Albee because our actor member had been in some Albee plays. As we did with poetry, we talked about the evolution of play writing in the U.S. and England and about how it has evolved from a regimented piece (with a beginning, a middle, a denouement, and a conclusion to tie up the loose ends) to the Theater of the Absurd writers, where nothing seems to happen and the characters and plot remain static. If I had had more time, I would probably have read *Waiting for Godot* by Samuel Becket (1954) with them.

The Writing

From the second week on, we conducted the "Writers' Workshop" in earnest. The rules for workshopping were minimal: Students had to be honest, specific, and appropriate about the work.

One of the girls, Katy, brought a poem, which I copied for everyone, and we spent about 15 minutes analyzing it. The fact that someone was willing to go first and expose herself to the scrutiny of others testified to the positive feel the group had for one another. Katy began by reading the poem while others made notes. They then took turns discussing the theme, the mood, and the language, pointing out words they felt were too vague and complimenting lines they found particularly powerful.

Katy's willingness to be the guinea pig opened the way for the others. For the rest of the sessions, there were always one or two pieces that students were willing to share for analysis.

Katy's willingness to share with others began what I found to be the most rewarding part of the workshop: an opportunity for students to critique at a very high level work in which they had invested time and effort. As they got to know each other better, they were willing not only to listen to the criticism of others, but also to defend what they felt they wanted to keep. They also learned the techniques of appropriate criticism. Sometimes, the group (including me) was held spellbound by the quality of the writing; at other times, it was just something to share as part of the obligation of participation. However, regardless of the quality, the maturity and seriousness with which all the students approached the work was both impressive and consistent.

At the end of the school year, and by the request of the students, I notified the two high schools they would be attending about their participation in the group. Because they would have the opportunity to participate in other writing venues, such as the literary magazine and the school newspapers, and since English classes at the high schools are leveled, I assured them that they would be likely to find a group of students with similar literary interests. The high schools responded by arranging for the students to be placed in the same English class, allowing them to continue their friendships and interests away from the less sympathetic eyes of their classmates.

Conclusions

In retrospect, I would say that this group was one of the most rewarding I've worked with in my many years of teaching. First, they destroyed the stereotype of "middle school student" forever in my mind. They were focused, motivated, and willing to give of themselves in a way that even many adults find difficult. When given something to read in an anthology, they often went beyond the assignment, reading the whole book if it appealed to them. They were able to stay on task remarkably well. Once, when I was late, they began the group without me, rather than waiting for me to appear. The boy/girl problems I had heard about from those who work in middle schools never materialized; they were more adult than many of the high school students I know.

The group clearly reflected the philosophy of the National Middle School Association, as did the principal and regular language arts teachers, who were certainly "sensitive to individual differences" and responded to "the natural diversity present in middle level classrooms." The students achieved at a level far beyond expectations, proving that "young adolescents are capable of far more than adults often assume." Last, the school promoted "flexible organizational structure," allowing the students and me a regular time to meet.

The students' success in the workshop gave further credence to the conclusion reached by VanTassel-Baska, Johnson, Hughes, & Boyce (1996): "focused high-powered and integrated curriculum intervention in the language arts of even a relatively short duration can bring about important changes in students' performance" (p. 474). The students fully met two of VanTassel-Baska et al.'s suggested outcomes: (a) literary analysis and interpretation outcomes and (b) linguistic competency outcomes (pp. 466–67). In terms of growth and sophistication in creative writing venues, notably short stories and poetry, the students' skills progressed greatly. They were also able to bring back some of the techniques of discussion to their classrooms, and the regular classroom teachers incorporated some of their ideas into the regular program. An unintended outcome was that the students were happier about school and were, therefore, better able to handle the demands of the regular program.

Perhaps the best part of the experience was helping me to understand how far gifted students can go if they are given the opportunity to do so. Their depth, perception, motivation, and ability to make connections were far greater than I had expected. They represented to me the best in intrinsic learning, as they wanted to read and discuss for its own sake, rather than for the grade. Their desire to continue this kind of workshop translated into active participation in their high schools' literary magazines. In both of the high schools, former students in the group became editors. Interestingly, in both high schools, they gave workshop contributions in much the same way that we did in the writers' workshop in eighth grade.

This group could serve as a model for other teachers of the gifted or for teachers who want the opportunity to work in-depth with selected students. Their joy, focus, and commitment all demonstrate to skeptics that such students are capable of deep, focused concentration.

References

Albee, E. (1961). *The American dream and the zoo story: Two plays by Edward Albee*. New York: Signet Books.

Ashbery, J. (1986). *Selected poems of John Ashbery*. New York: Viking.

Beckett, S. (1954). *Waiting for Godot: A tragicomedy in two acts*. New York: Grove Press.

Berrigan, T. (1994). *Selected poems by Ted Berrigan*. New York: Penguin.

Carnegie Corporation. (1989). *Turning points: Preparing American youth for the 21st century: The report of the task force on education of young adolescents*. New York: Author.

Frost, R. (1979). *Poems of Robert Frost: The collected poems, complete, and unabridged*. New York: Henry Holt Paper.

Henry, O. (1991). *41 stories by O. Henry*. New York: New American Library.

Ibsen, H. (1969). *Four great plays by Ibsen*. New York: Bantam Books.

Jackson, S. (1992). *The lottery and other stories*. New York: Noonday Press.

National Middle School Association (NMSA). (1995). *This we believe: Developmentally responsive middle level schools*. Columbus, OH: Author.

Norton, J., & Gretton, F. (1972). *Writing incredibly short plays, poems, stories*. New York: Harcourt Brace Jovanovich.

Plucker, J., & McIntire, J. (1996). Academic survivability in high-potential, middle school students. *Gifted Child Quarterly, 40*, 7–14.

Poe, E. A. (1999). *The pit and the pendulum and other stories*. New York: Viking Children's Books.

Robinson, E. A. (1973). *Introduction to the poem*. Rochelle Park, NJ: Hayden Book.

Smith, E. (1999). Middle school: The balancing act. *Communicator, 30*, 12–13.

Swenson, M. (1978). How everything happens (based on the study of the wave). In K. Gensler & N. Nyhart (Eds.), *The poetry connection*. New York: Teachers and Writers Collaborative.

VanTassel-Baska, J., Johnson, D., Hughes, C., & Boyce, L. (1996). A study of language arts curriculum effectiveness with gifted learners. *Journal for the Education of the Gifted, 10,* 461–480.

Vonnegut, K. (1968). *Welcome to the monkey house.* New York: Dell.

Wilder, T. (1957). *Three plays: Our Town, Skin of Our Teeth, Matchmaker.* New York: Avon Books

Williams, W. C. (1978). This is just to say. In K. Gensler & N. Nyhart (Eds.), *The poetry connection.* New York: Teachers and Writers Collaborative.

Author Note

Most of these short stories, poems, and plays are in anthologies. I have included sources where they can be found. One caveat: Choose what you love and what the students love, not necessarily what I've listed.

chapter 12

R.I.T.E. Reading

constructing meaning by finding what's
"wrong" in an informational text

by **Keith Polette**

> *"The gift of reading, like all natural gifts,*
> *must be nourished or it will atrophy."*
> —Katherine Paterson

if the "gift of reading" is to flourish for gifted and talented students, it must, as Katherine Paterson says, be "nourished." And, while it is true that gifted and talented students usually have little trouble reading, especially in the areas that interest them, many of them need further guidance when it comes to developing strategies that lead to deeper levels of comprehension and enjoyment. If we are to offer such guidance and nourishment, we must give our students regular doses of metacognitive "vitamins" and rhetorical "minerals." These vitamins and minerals are especially important in supporting the ways students learn to grapple with, and thus make sense of, informational texts.

Frequently, when students are assigned to read an informational text, especially one that is unrelated to their interests, they tend to skim it without deriving much enjoyment. When they skim, they are not exercising full, strategic control over their reading. As such, students often read an assigned informational text as if it is unrelated to their prior knowledge, to their previous experience, and to a variety of purposes that could inform their reading. Consequently, students may indeed ferret out a few nuggets of factual data as they read, but they may fail to put those data into a larger context that is both personally rewarding and academically important.

R.I.T.E.

R.I.T.E. is an acronym for a reading process that occurs in four stages: Read, Interrogate, Tell, Explore. It enables students to use a multifaceted approach to develop the kinds of critical reading skills necessary for constructing meaning as they read an informational text. As such, R.I.T.E. enables students to see how an informational text is a site where meaning can be created in a multistaged, dialectical process. As students engage in the process of the R.I.T.E. activity, they use fluent and flexible thinking to make thoughtful predictions prior to reading the text and then employ close observation skills to search for specific information as they read. Furthermore, students use analytical skills to determine if the information in the text is relevant to their needs. Finally, they adopt synthetic skills to assimilate and accommodate information they found in the text into their internal rhetorical structures.

R.I.T.E. is also centered on the idea that reading must be fun and that pedagogical activities must contain, when possible, elements of play. Vygotsky (1978) reminds us that play is a key trait of successful education.

> [P]*lay gives a child a new form of desires*. It teaches her to desire by relating her desires to a fictitious 'I,' to her role in the game and its rules. In this way a child's greatest achievements are possible in play, achievements that tomorrow will become her basic level of real action and morality. (p. 100, emphasis in original)

R.I.T.E. initiates just such a sense of play into the process of reading an informational text because it makes new achievements and

- How many of the following do you know something about?
- Do you know, or can you guess, where each is located?
- Which one would you like to visit?
- Which would you not like to visit?
- What do they all have in common?

_____ Egyptian Pyramids	_____ Statue of Liberty
_____ Greek Parthenon	_____ St. Louis Arch
_____ Sistine Chapel	_____ Great Wall of China
_____ Leaning Tower of Pisa	_____ Big Ben
_____ Mount Rushmore	_____ Stonehenge
_____ Eiffel Tower	_____ Egyptian Sphinx
_____ Aztec Pyramids	

Figure 12.1. **Prereading activity**

actions possible. By playing with the text, students also take cognitive and imaginative risks as they construct meaning. As such, the activity encourages students to imagine what an informational text is, how they might approach it, and how they might use it.

R.I.T.E. in Action

The following is an example of how R.I.T.E. can be used to enable upper-elementary and middle-school students to enlist critical thinking skills and to develop a desire to read an article about Mount Rushmore.

The first step involves an oral, prereading activity that orients students toward the Rushmore article (see Figure 12.1). The ensuing discussion enables students to articulate what they know and what they think they know about each item. Because "right answers" are not the focus, students will enjoy the freedom to offer divergent answers and to entertain new, and sometimes contradictory, ideas.

Moreover, the discussion, which may last 10–20 minutes, will stimulate students' curiosity. Because no "right answers" to the questions are supplied by the teacher and because every answer students give (no matter how divergent) is acceptable, students find the necessary time to speculate, consider, and inquire. That is, they find themselves at the headwaters of a self-generated "need to know." If students are to let their natural curiosity surface, then they need a stretch of time to think and discuss.

The next step involves narrowing the discussion to the topic of Mount Rushmore, which might involve the following discussion questions:

- Who do you think sculpted the faces onto Mount Rushmore?
- What techniques and tools do you think the sculptor used?
- When do you think the faces were sculpted?
- Where do you think Mount Rushmore is located?
- Why do you think the sculptor decided to create the monument?
- How long do you think it took to complete the monument?

As before, students should speculate about possible answers and, if need be, guess. Because this part of the prereading activity is based on open-ended questions, it is important to encourage students to use fluent thinking and offer as many answers as possible. Students should also be encouraged to use flexible thinking so that their answers range broadly and widely. When invited to use these two different thinking skills to speculate about questions prior to reading, students usually become energized, interested, and curious.

During the second discussion, the answers students come up with should be written on the blackboard or on an overhead transparency. When finished, it is a good idea to pause and wait. This allows suspense to build. Feeling the tension, students often ask which of their answers are correct. This is the point to distribute copies of the article entitled "Mount Rushmore: Four Faces that Rock" (see Figure 12.2) and inform students that they might find the answers they are seeking in the article.

Step 1: Read

Prepared for Step 1 of R.I.T.E. (Read), students are ready to become self-directed, critical readers. One problem that stu-

---

Mount Rushmore: Four Faces That Rock!

Named after New York attorney John Jacob Rushé, Mount Rushmore is located in the Blue Hills of the Wabash Mountain Range in northwestern North Dakota. The faces originally intended to be carved into the mountain were not those of the presidents, but rather three American heroes: John Colter, Kit Carson, and Buffalo "Bill" Cody.

The mammoth sculpture of the presidents was initiated in 1919 by Gutzon Borglum and completed in 1953. (Borglum's grandson finished the last year's work after Borglum's death in 1952). The project cost just under $500,000. On the mountainside are carved the heads of Presidents Washington, Adams, Lincoln, and Truman.

Borglum first created a working drawing of the project; he then laid out the measurements on the 12,000 foot high face of the mountain's Wilderness Peak. The appropriate areas were subsequently demolished by cannon fire. Afterward, men were lowered in seats from the top of the mountain to sculpt the rock with large electric drills and chisels.

The sculpture is so large that it is visible from a distance of 150 miles. The heads of the presidents are carved to the scale of a person who is 835 feet tall. This means the head of Washington is 155 feet from chin to hairline and the eye of Adams is large enough to hold 17 adults!

The North Dakota Department of Tourism estimates that 25,000 people visit Mount Rushmore each year.

As a direct result of Borglum's work, architects in England are now planning a similar project: to etch the faces of Harold I, Richard III, Henry V, and Elizabeth I on the peak of Scafell Pike (elevation: 3,210 feet) in the Lake District. Although a number of fringe, antiroyalist groups have been attempting to stop the project, it is scheduled to begin in 2010.

To date, the Queen's only comment about the brewing controversy has been, "We shall not be swayed from making faces on the Pike."

—Jules Verne

Figure 12.2. **Article with incorrect data**

dents frequently experience when reading assigned informational texts is that they become overwhelmed with data. Because they have no clear, self-generated purpose for reading, they often fail to distinguish between what is important in the text and what is not.

The two prereading discussions help students decide what they should notice as they read. Specifically, the answers students give to the discussion questions and, most notably, the answers that pertained to Mount Rushmore become guides for students as they read. When they speculate and guess about information that may be contained in a text they are going to read, they naturally want to find a way to verify their own ideas. In this way, they develop a "need to know," and their reading is then driven by two specific, well-defined, self-generated purposes: (a) compare data in the text with their speculations and (b) find out if they were correct.

As the students begin reading the article, the teacher should ask them after a minute or two to stop. At this point, the following announcement should be delivered: "Many of the facts in the article are incorrect!" Ask the students to resume reading and identify any facts that appear to be incorrect.

Step 2: Interrogate

The interrogation stage of R.I.T.E. is crucial, for it allows students to query the article dynamically. Robert and Michelle Root-Bernstein (1999) remind us that "all knowledge begins in observation" (p. 31). As students read the article, they are not simply locating facts, but also weighing the veracity of each fact they locate. As such, they are entering into a new reading game and are necessarily changing the speed and depth of their reading. Additionally, they are using the skill of close observation in their encounter with new stimuli to both increase and challenge their knowledge base. Langer (1997) wrote, "we can present novel stimuli to our students. We can introduce material through games, because in games players vary their responses to . . . look more closely at all aspects of the situation" (p. 42). Because R.I.T.E. may be a novel game as Langer describes, students will need to shift their cognitive footing. They can't proceed in their reading as they had done before because the linguistic playing field and rules have changed and there are new problems to solve. de Bono (1990) reminds us that "in problem solving one always assumes certain boundaries" (p. 93). The same is true with reading: It is hemmed by boundaries that are based on the nature of the text and on the reader's skills and expectations. If we are to initiate changes in the way a reader reads, we must change either the text or the reader's expectations—or, if possible, both. When students read the Rushmore article, they will need to shift their expectations because the text is not the kind they have usually encountered before. Consequently, they need to slow down in order to question and evaluate each piece of data they encounter.

Evaluation in this case takes the form of further questions. For instance, students might ask:

- Is this fact true?
- What evidence in the article would lead me to believe the fact is either true or false?
- Is there any way, within the limits of the article, to test the truthfulness of the fact?
- What do I know about Mount Rushmore or about the fact itself that would lead me to think it is true or false?

These kinds of questions are the general criteria upon which students should base their critical thinking. By using the questions as tools, students are free to think about, discuss (in small groups), and weigh each fact.

Lively group discussions often ensue at this stage of R.I.T.E as students try to differentiate between fact and nonfact. After all, "Noticing new things about any body of information is involving. When students draw distinctions, the distinctions are necessarily relevant to them. Distinctions reveal that the material is situated in a context and imply that other contexts may be considered" (Langer, 1997, p. 75). As they read, students draw distinctions between what seems to be true and what seems to be in error—the more distinctions they draw, the more involved they become.

For instance, students might discuss the following point: "The faces originally intended to be carved into the mountain were not those of the presidents, but rather three American heroes: John Colter, Kit Carson, and Buffalo 'Bill' Cody." Some students may be adamant that the entire statement is incorrect. They may give such reasons as

- Who ever heard of those guys, especially John Colter?
- If somebody was going make an American monument about famous people, it would have to be about the Presidents, not about people no one has ever heard of.

Other students may counter with:

- Maybe the monument was just some guy's idea and he liked those "heroes."
- Maybe he was eccentric and didn't plan on the monument becoming as famous as it has become.
- Maybe he didn't like politics and didn't want to carve the Presidents.

Students tend to take positions that are supported not so much by prior knowledge, but by inferences, associations, and assumptions. One reason why the article is effective is because most students have little or no prior knowledge about Mount Rushmore. Moreover, because the article is "inverted" (full of errors, not truths), students will be able think about information in new ways. "It may be that by inverting . . . we free ourselves from preconceived categories and open ourselves to the available information" (Langer, 1997, p. 133). Freed from preconceived notions about how this informational text functions and what its purposes are, students must think critically and carefully as they evaluate each fact. The goal is not for students to arrive at what they know, but at what they think they know. Moreover, it was also important for students to give voice to how they arrived at what they think they know. As R. Hunt (1993) mentioned, "for language to be meaningful it must be the vehicle for social transaction" (p. 114). As students talk about why they think certain facts are true or false, they situate themselves in metacognitive reflection, a key element to critical thought and to the construction of socially configured meaning.

Step 3: Tell

Once students draw distinctions between what they think is true and false in the article, they are ready to share their findings. Their findings, though, should be confined only to what they think is incorrect in the article. In this way, they need to proceed through the article line by line to identify what they thought were errors. As they do, the teacher's job is to cross out any fact students thought were nonfacts (the article should be placed on a transparency). It is a good idea to tell them that, as

Mount Rushmore: Four Faces that Rock!

Named after ~~New York attorney John Jacob Rushé~~, Mount Rushmore is located in the ~~Blue Hills~~ of the ~~Wabash Mountain Range~~ in northwestern ~~North Dakota~~. The faces originally intended to be carved into the mountain were not those of the presidents, but rather ~~three American heroes: John Colter, Kit Carson, and Buffalo "Bill" Cody.~~

The mammoth sculpture of the presidents was initiated in ~~1919 by Gutzon Borglum~~ and completed in ~~1953~~. (Borglum's grandson finished the last year's work after Borglum's death in 1952). The project cost just under ~~$500,000~~. On the mountainside are carved the heads of Presidents Washington, ~~Adams~~, Lincoln, and ~~Truman~~.

Borglum first created a working drawing of the project; he then laid out the measurements on the ~~12,000~~ foot high face of the mountain's ~~Wilderness Peak~~. The appropriate areas were subsequently demolished by ~~cannon fire~~. Afterwards, men were lowered in seats from the top of the mountain to sculpt the rock with ~~large electric drills~~ and chisels.

The sculpture is so large that it is visible from a distance of ~~150 miles~~. The heads of the presidents are carved to the scale of a person who is ~~835~~ feet tall. This means the head of Washington is ~~155~~ feet from chin to hairline and the eye of ~~Adams~~ is large enough to hold ~~17 adults~~!

The ~~North Dakota~~ Department of Tourism estimates that ~~25,000~~ people visit Mount Rushmore each year.

As a direct result of Borglum's work, architects in England are now planning a similar project: to etch the faces of ~~Harold I~~, Richard III, Henry V, and Elizabeth I on the peak of ~~Scafell Pike~~ (elevation: 3,210 feet) in the Lake District. ~~Although a number of fringe, antiroyalist groups have been attempting to stop the project~~, it is scheduled to begin in ~~2010~~.

~~To date, the Queen's only comment about the brewing controversy has been, "We shall not be swayed from making faces on the Pike."~~

—~~Jules Verne~~

**Figure 12.3. Data crossed out
that students thought were incorrect**

you cross out facts, you will not state whether the facts are true or false (see Figure 12.3). Tell them, also, that you will cross out anything they tell you to (one exception is not to cross out entire paragraphs).

The "Tell" stage is important because it gives every student a chance to express a thought and take a risk. Because students aren't sure if their ideas are correct, they have to take risks when they suggest items to cross out. The risks, however, became part of the "reading game" of the activity. And, because students experience the activity as a game, they will be willing to take part in it. The activity-as-game also encourages students to relax, let down their guards, and discover more fluid ways of thinking and participating. Not only are students sharing their well-wrought speculations, but they are also creating a classroom dynamic based on cooperation, participation, and curiosity. When these three elements combine, learning soars.

Step 4: Explore

After the students finish suggesting items to cross out, they are ready to measure their accuracy. In fact, at this point in the activity, students are usually hungry for the right answers. Such a need, based on cognitive and emotional involvement, is crucial if students are going to engage actively the correct Rushmore article. Such a need also signals the difference between passive and active reading. When such a need is in place, students will then have a clear, self-generated purpose for reading: to find out what the correct information is, to see how closely their speculations match the correct data, and to be surprised.

As soon as they get the article (see Figure 12.4), they begin reading—usually without encouragement. The whole point of the R.I.T.E. activity is to motivate students to want to read the accurate version of the Rushmore article. As they read the article, they naturally engage in comparative thinking. They compare the items they had wanted to be deleted from the first article with their counterparts in the second article. By comparing data, students are also performing a critical reading task. They will use the fewest possible clues in the text to create meaning. As the students read the accurate article, they read selectively, carefully, critically, and energetically.

From R.I.T.E. to Write

After reading and discussing both articles, the teacher should then invite students to use both Mount Rushmore arti-

Mount Rushmore: Four Faces that Rock!

Named after New York attorney **Charles E. Rushmore**, Mount Rushmore is located in the **Black Hills** of **southwestern South Dakota**. The faces originally intended to be carved into the mountain were not those of the presidents, but rather three American heroes: Kit Carson, Jim Bridger, and John Colter. The mammoth sculpture of the presidents was initiated in **1929** by Gutzon Borglum and completed in **1942**; it cost **$1 million**. (Borglum's son finished the last year's work after Borglum's death in 1941). On the mountainside are carved the heads of Presidents Washington, **Jefferson**, Lincoln, and **Theodore Roosevelt.**

Borglum first created a **scale model** of the project; he then laid out the measurements on the **6,200** foot high face of the mountain's Wilderness Peak. The appropriate areas were demolished by **dynamite**. Men were then lowered in seats from the top of the mountain to sculpt the rock with **compressed air drills** and chisels.

The mountain sculpture is so large that it is visible from a distance of **60 miles**. The heads of the presidents are carved to the scale of a person who is **465 feet tall**. That means that the head of Washington is **60 feet** from chin to hairline and that the eye of **Jefferson** is large enough to hold **1 adult**.

NB: **The last two paragraphs in the first version were fictitious.**

The facts for the correct version were found in *Panati's Extraordinary Origins of Everyday Things*, pp. 282–284.

Figure 12.3. **Correct version with corrected facts in bold**

cles as models for their own research and writing. Students should select one item from the list (see Figure 12.1), research it, and then write an error-ridden and an accurate article. The purpose is to have students share their erroneous articles with the class, who then tries to ascertain which statements in the article are incorrect. The students who wrote the articles then share the correct versions. Based on the R.I.T.E. activity, students become teacher-experts on a particular topic.

Moreover, by writing and sharing their own articles based on the R.I.T.E. activity, students will find an important way to enhance their literacy development by making the reading-writing connection. Such a connection results in productive thinking, which is grounded in the dynamics of synthesis; "productive thought occurs when internal imagination and external experience coincide" (Root-Bernstein & Root-Bernstein, 1999, p. 24). As students construct their various articles, they blend their external experiences (accurate information) and internal imagination (fictive data) in ways that are unique, individual, and delightful.

After students research their topics by investigating at least two different informational texts, they create articles packed with misleading information. In order to create their articles, however, they have to understand the purposes of their writing, which is to inform and to mislead. They also have to confront concerns of content by changing correct information to incorrect and by adding sentences and paragraphs that contain false information. They also need to be concerned with the elements of style because the article they construct must have a journalistic, objective tone. Furthermore, they will need to be cognizant of matters of organization and structure as they arrange information (which should be grouped under subtopics, such as location, purposes, designer, cost, visitors, etc.) into logically organized paragraphs.

Students have created wonderful articles with titles such as "The St. Louis Arch: The Design That Inspired a Hamburger Chain"; "Big Ben: The Clock That Time Forgot"; "The Leaning Tower of Pisa: The Building's Right, The World's Wrong"; and "The Great Wall of China: Stacks of Dinner Plates That Saved a Nation."

Students will certainly enjoy the R.I.T.E. activity. But, more importantly, they will learn to negotiate the reading and writing of informational texts—two yoked skills that nourish the gift of literacy.

References

de Bono, E. (1990). *Lateral thinking*. New York: Harper & Row.

Hunt, R. (1993). Texts, tabloids, and utterances: Writing and reading for meaning in and out of the classroom. In S. B. Straw & D. Bogdan (Eds.), *Constructive reading* (pp. 113–129). Portsmouth, NH: Boynton/Cook.

Langer, E. (1997). *The power of mindful learning*. Reading, MA: Addison-Wesley.

Panati, C. (1987). *Extraordinary origins of everyday things.* New York: Harper & Row.

Root-Bernstein, R., & Root-Bernstein, M. (1999). *Sparks of genius.* New York: Houghton Mifflin.

Vygotsky, L. S. (1978). *Mind in society.* Cambridge, MA: Harvard University Press.

About the Authors

Sheila R. Alber is an associate professor in the Department of Curriculum, Instruction, and Special Education at The University of Southern Mississippi.

Sharon Black teaches advanced writing and research and methods for teaching writing at the David O. McKay School of Education at Brigham Young University.

Donna Y. Ford is Betts Chair of Education and Human Development at Peabody College, Vanderbilt University. Her work focuses on gifted diverse students, urban education, and multicultural curriculum. She has written several books and articles and consults with school districts nationally.

Cecile Parris Frey has an extensive background as a teacher of gifted and talented children and as a supervisor of gifted support programs. Author of the publication, *A Gifted Program that Works*, Dr. Frey completed her Ed.D., M.S., and A.B. degrees at the University of Pennsylvania. Her areas of expertise include English and social studies methods, gifted underachievers and dually identified students, and gender issues in the classroom.

Deidra M. Gammill is a doctoral student in adult education and literacy studies at The University of Southern Mississippi.

J. John Harris III is currently professor of educational law in the College of Education, scholar in the African American Studies and Research Program in the College of Arts and Sciences, and vice chair of the President's Commission on Diversity at the University of Kentucky. His research interest lies in educational law and urban gifted education.

Tyrone C. Howard is assistant professor of social studies and global education in the College of Education at The Ohio State University.

Bertie Kingore is a national consultant who has worked with students, their teachers, and their parents for more than 30 years. The author of numerous articles, instructional aids, and 20 books on education, she is currently a consultant for Professional Associates Publishing.

Andrew P. Johnson is professor and chair of the Department of Educational Studies: Special Populations at Minnesota State University, Mankato. He specializes in holistic education, spiritual intelligence, literacy instruction, action research, strategies for inclusive classrooms, and gifted education.

Christa M. Martin is a doctoral student in special education at The University of Southern Mississippi

Shannon O'Day is a teacher of the gifted in Paulding County, Georgia.

Keith Polette is an associate professor and director of the English Education program in the Department of English at the University of Texas at El Paso. His most recent publications are *Read and Write It Out Loud: Guided Oral Literacy Strategies* and *Isabel and the Hungry Coyote*, a bilingual children's book.

Robert W. Seney is a professor of gifted studies at the Mississippi University for Women, the coordinator of graduate programs in education, and the director of the Mississippi Governor's School. He is active in the World Council for Gifted Children and is currently serving as the chair for the 2005 World Conference.

Andrea Vosslamber is a doctoral student at Massey University in New Zealand, where she also works as a literacy adviser to schools.

Anita Winstead is a primary teacher at King Elementary School in Louisville, Kentucky. She teaches gifted students in a multiple-abilities classroom.

Printed in the United States
by Baker & Taylor Publisher Services